VALIDATED

Add Value. Build Trust. Be Seen.

Knox

Knox Keith

Jacket hardback ISBN: 979-8-9941948-0-5

Hardback ISBN: 979-8-9941948-2-9

eBook ISBN: 979-8-9941948-1-2

Cover and interior design by meadencreative.com

First Edition

Printed in the United States

Contents

Preface

Why This Book Exists

Here's the concept behind this book: You have a professional problem! Before people meet you, they will Google you. (Or AI you or "search you up." Apparently that's a Gen Alpha saying.) But I'm sticking with Google, even if it dates me.

Every day, there are 8.5 billion name searches conducted on Google!

Before a job interview, sales meeting, or board presentation, someone has already typed your name into a search bar. In an instant, they are forming an opinion about you, deciding whether to lean in or move on without you even being in the room.

So, the question is when they search for you, what will they find?

We live in an era where your *digital footprint* is your first impression. Digital footprints are the collection of search results, social profiles, articles, videos, images, and traces of past activity that follow your name online. It's the modern equivalent of a handshake, resume, and reference letter combined, but it's often unplanned, unmanaged, and dated.

And that's a problem. For most people, it's not intentional.

The Reputation Precedent

When I was growing up, my mother and grandmother often said, "Your reputation precedes you." In the analog world, that meant neighbors, teachers, and colleagues had formed an opinion based on what they'd heard or seen—for better or worse.

Reputation was built through consistent action and the stories people told about you. In small towns and tight-knit communities, credibility was your currency. You were hired, trusted, or referred based on character and word of mouth.

Fast forward to today: The principle hasn't changed, but the scale has. Your "neighbors" now include recruiters, investors, clients, and colleagues across time zones—all of whom are just one Google search away. Your reputation still precedes you, but now it travels globally, instantly, and is on your permanent record (for those of us old enough to remember those words of warning!).

The Stakes in the Digital Age

Your digital footprint answers, or fails to answer, three critical questions for anyone considering you for an opportunity:

- Is this person credible?
- Can I trust them?
- Are they the right fit?

I say this because I've seen executives win and lose multimillion-dollar deals because of what showed up (or didn't) when someone Googled them.

(We'll discuss this further in a case study.) I have also personally landed unadvertised six-figure contracts because my digital presence confirmed my expertise before I even walked into the room.

Yet most professionals, entrepreneurs, students, small businesses, and nonprofits are not taking full advantage of the free, high-impact tools available to them, especially on LinkedIn.

Outside Perspective

"Influence is the ability to get someone to take action."

—Amanda Russell, *The Influencer Code*

On LinkedIn, that action might be to consider you for an interview, comment on your post, engage in a conversation, or provide a referral.

Influence isn't about vanity metrics—such as number of followers. Influence is about credibility and action. *Social proof*, or in this case, *digital proof*, is the signal that establishes trust.

A Common Problem

Here's what I've observed after analyzing more than 10,000 LinkedIn profiles:

- Most have only the bare minimum filled in: a job title, a few bullet points, or maybe an outdated headshot.
- Activity is sporadic at best, often limited to posting only when job hunting.
- Few have a content strategy or clear subject matter focus.

That means they are invisible in the very place where 95 percent of recruiters, potential clients, and decision-makers are looking.

Why This Book

This book exists to help you fix that. It helps you become intentionally visible in a professional setting.

It's about creating something I call Digital Validation™, a strong, consistent, professional online presence that establishes trust before you ever say a word or meet a person.

In this book, you will learn to position yourself as a subject matter expert, expand your visibility, and ensure that when people find you online, they see the version of you that aligns with your professional goals and capabilities.

The formulas and frameworks that you will find in this book work. I've built them from more than two decades as a management consultant, working with Fortune 500 companies, start-ups, nonprofits, MBA students, sales teams, mid-level managers, and executives. The process is the same whether you're a CEO or just starting out and whether you work for a Fortune 500 company or a small business. The process has worked for my clients, students, friends, colleagues, and me, so I know it will work for you.

A Framework That Works

At times throughout this book, I will reference my Strategic Effects framework, a repeatable process I use in consulting to build knowledge, credibility, visibility, and results.

1. **Observe**—Gather the facts, data, and signals.
2. **Orient**—Put those facts in context.
3. **Analyze**—Find patterns and leverage points.
4. **Act**—Take intentional, measurable steps.
5. **Repeat**—Learn, adapt, and continue.

You do not have to memorize this. Just know that it's the structure guiding every chapter, exercise, and case study ahead. It's an approach that can help you see things that you may not have seen before, giving you new insights. And it's a framework that is *kaizen* in its approach, one that is designed for continual improvements versus a set-it-and-leave-it mindset.

What's Ahead

Over the next chapters, you'll find:

- Case studies showing both wins and missed opportunities.
- Practical exercises to apply immediately.
- Frameworks and formulas for optimizing your LinkedIn presence and content strategy.
- Proven tactics for engaging online in a way that builds trust and drives opportunity.
- QR codes linking you to extra materials.

By the end, you will know how to be the publicist for your own career, intentionally shaping the professional story people find when they look you up. And you will know how to do so without sounding salesy or pushy.

Whether you're ready or not, your reputation is already out there. This book will help you take control of it.

Definitions

Throughout the book, I use many terms. If you are not already familiar with them, here's an introduction:

- Digital Footprints: The trail of your online content and interactions, as well as public records tied to your name; can be intentional or unintentional in nature.
- Digital Validation™: The intentional creation of a strong, consistent, professional presence that confirms your expertise.

- Digital Dis-Validation™: Choosing not to participate in platforms or conversations, thereby removing yourself from consideration.
- Content Pillars: The core topics about which you consistently post or comment on to build your professional brand.
- Sales Funnel: The path someone takes from first discovering you to becoming a customer. In its simplest form:
    - ▸ Awareness (They know you exist.)
    - ▸ to Consideration (They're deciding whether you're the right fit.)
    - ▸ to Purchase (They say yes.)

Statistics

- LinkedIn:
    - ▸ 1.2 billion registered users.
        - » Only 26 percent log in in monthly.
        - » Only 11 percent log in daily.
        - » 95 percent of recruiters actively look for candidates on LinkedIn.
- Facebook:
    - ▸ 3.7 billion registered users.
        - » 69 percent log in daily.
- Instagram:
    - ▸ 2 billion registered users.
    - ▸ 25 percent log in daily.
- TikTok:
    - ▸ 1.6 billion registered users.
        - » 57 percent log in daily.

- August 2025 minutes per day on each social media platform:
  - TikTok—56 minutes.
  - Instagram—33 minutes.
  - Facebook—31 minutes.
  - YouTube—19 minutes.
  - Pinterest—14 minutes.
  - LinkedIn—7 minutes.

Exercises

1. Time to do a Google name search on you! Go ahead, whip out your search engine and enter your name. [Note: People with more common names may have to leverage additional qualifiers such as the city where they live.] Go beyond the first page of the search results.
   - Write down what you find.
   - Are there random things in your search results? Is it positive? Negative? Neutral? Professional?
2. Do the same thing for LinkedIn.
3. Is it up-to-date? Is your headshot from this year? Is your current employer and role listed?

QR Code

Introduction: Your Reputation Precedes You

As I mentioned in the last chapter, growing up, I vividly remember my mother and grandmother telling me, "Your reputation precedes you."

It was one of those steadfast pieces of wisdom that felt almost like a commandment, something understood and rarely questioned. As a kid, I thought it simply meant people would know about me before I entered a room. If I had a reputation for being responsible, hardworking, or kind, that would arrive ahead of me. If I was careless or lazy, that would travel, too.

In the analog days of my childhood, reputation was built through community, word of mouth, and relationships forged over time. There were no LinkedIn profiles, curated Instagram feeds, or Google search results filled with articles, headshots, and interviews. Your reputation was shaped by your actions and the stories people told about you, and it moved through the world in conversations, not algorithms.

Reputation Then vs. Now

The idea that a reputation precedes a person isn't new. My mother and grandmother grew up in eras when a handshake could seal a deal, and being "from a good family" could open doors. In small towns and tight-knit communities, credibility was your currency.

Today, the principle hasn't changed, but the scale has. Your "neighbors" are now global. Your name can be searched, and you will be judged by people you've never met, in industries you haven't worked in yet—all at the speed of a Google search.

This raises three important questions:

- If someone Googles your name today, what story do they find?
- Are you actively shaping that story or leaving it to chance?
- Does your digital footprint align with who you are and who you want to be?

Why It Matters

In the analog world, reputation was relational, built through proximity and conversation.

In the digital world, it's exponential, built through visibility and proof.

Your online presence is now the first filter of trust.

It can determine whether doors open or stay closed and whether opportunities find you or pass you by.

The challenge is that most professionals treat their online presence as an afterthought, a static profile instead of a dynamic reputation engine.

That gap between *who you are* and *what people see* is where careers stall and credibility leaks.

This book closes that gap. It's about building proof and polish—substance that can be searched, trusted, and shared.

Case Study—The Tale of Two Executives (Part 1)

Let me introduce you to Joseph.

Joseph was a young executive—dynamic, charismatic, and ambitious. He had just taken a VP of sales role for one of our most profitable product lines at a large, high-tech manufacturer. The product was priced right, and his team was solid.

I traveled with him for a high-stakes pitch to a major East Coast company. Everything suggested the deal was ours and that the meeting was just a formality. The meeting went well, the presentation hit the mark, and we even celebrated over dinner thinking it was a done deal.

Then … silence. We got ghosted before *ghosting* was a term! Weeks later, we learned that we had lost the deal.

During my follow-up calls, a contact from the client's purchasing department explained:

"When we Googled Joseph, we found nothing."

No LinkedIn presence. No industry associations. No thought leadership. His lack of a visible, credible digital footprint made him a perceived liability. And, they feared that Joseph was likely to leave for a new role in a year or two.

The supplier they chose had a VP of sales who was active and respected in the industry. His LinkedIn profile was rich with articles and commentary. He contributed to conversations online and was visible at conferences. In short, his digital presence preceded him and helped win the deal.

In terms of definitions, Joseph led me to coin the term *Digital Dis-Validation*™, when someone intentionally takes an inactive stance online—avoiding professional platforms, declining to share expertise, and ignoring engagement opportunities—that disqualifies them from opportunities. It's not neutral. It is a clear choice that can cost you.

Welcome to the Age of Digital Validation™: The New Reputation Currency

This is where Digital Validation™ comes into play. Forget *personal branding.* (I'll go into this in greater depth in a future chapter.) Personal branding is about flash and is limited to only broadcasting messages. That is, you only post and never engage.

In terms of the sales funnel (which we will go into at greater length later), personal branding is limited to trying to garner awareness.

There are three stages of the sales funnel:

- Awareness
- Consideration
- Purchase

Professional branding, the focus of this book, means doing more than just grabbing attention. It is built on adding value consistently over time. It is about being intentional with your posts. It is about building connections and nurturing relationships so that you establish *trust.* You are viewed as credible and as someone whose thoughts and insights are valued, so people naturally move with you from awareness to consideration to purchase.

Here's another way to say it: *Personal branding* is surface level; *Professional branding* has depth (and purpose and meaning).

Your *professional digital presence* requires time, attention, strategy, and intentionality. By being more intentional, you can ensure that when someone Googles you, they will see a professional version of you that includes all the things you want them to see, one that is polished and reflects what you are doing or want to do in your career.

To summarize, *Digital Validation*™ is building a strong, consistent, and professional online presence. This book is designed to help you do just that: give you the tools and frameworks to help you be proactive in creating that professional digital presence.

That means doing the following:

- Optimizing your LinkedIn profile to reflect your expertise.
- Staying active on the platform.
- Sharing valuable content that positions you as a subject matter expert or thought leader.
- Engaging with others in a way that builds credibility.
- Being intentional about the digital footprint that you leave behind.

Where This Book Will Take You

In order to build a strong, consistent, and professional online presence, we will methodically work through a proven framework.

Here are the steps of the framework:

- Analyze your current LinkedIn presence through my proprietary LinkedIn Scorecard.
- Optimize your LinkedIn profile, so it works as your professional storefront.
- Create a content strategy that positions you as a subject matter expert.
- Engage online in ways that build relationships, not just impressions.
- Learn to think like a publicist for your own career.

You will also hear from other voices—leaders, authors, and practitioners—whose perspectives reinforce the strategies we'll explore. And you will see ample case studies as well as exercises to complete.

Your Role in the Process

In the end, you don't need to post every day or aim for viral content, but you do need to be intentional. By investing in your digital presence, you can control the version of yourself the world sees, one that reflects your current expertise and your future goals.

You are your greatest asset. When you invest accordingly, opportunities will find you.

In the chapters ahead, we'll identify the current state of your digital footprint and then build it into an asset that opens doors, builds trust, and creates opportunity.

If you want to differentiate yourself, stand out from the crowd, or develop your voice to position yourself as a subject matter expert (SME) or thought leader, then keep reading. Do the exercises and homework. Invest time on platforms like LinkedIn instead of mindlessly dooms scrolling on other platforms.

Outside Perspective ...

Joseph's story isn't about social media vanity metrics. It's about trust. Visibility alone doesn't equal influence.

Amanda Russell, author of *The Influencer Code*, defines true influence as follows:

Influence = Awareness + Trust + Benevolence

As she states, "True influence is the ability to get someone to act."

Her point—one that is fundamental—is that benevolence is what separates authentic influence from manipulation.

Benevolence is a genuine disposition to do good: kindness, goodwill, and a desire to promote the well-being of others. It can show up as an act of generosity, a moment of empathy, or simply an intent to add value.

In the early days of social media, the rule was simple: Share good stuff.

That idea still holds true, although we don't see as much of it as we should. It's not enough to be seen. You have to become *credible.* You have to be *trusted.* Trust is our digital currency. You have to be perceived as working in the best interest of others.

Our goal then as businesses and individuals should be to cultivate sincere relationships that inspire action, not just attention.

This is where my philosophy comes in: Add value.

When we post, comment, or share online, the majority of what we do should be focused on *adding value* to others by offering insights, perspective, encouragement, or education. The return isn't in the likes. The return is in the goodwill and trust we build over time.

We will explore this concept more deeply in the chapters around content, where we will look at how to consistently create and share material that informs, inspires, or helps your audience move forward.

** For more on Amanda Russell, see the QR Code at the end of the chapter with links to our interview during #SxSW 2024.

Who am I?

I've spent the last two decades helping executives, entrepreneurs, and organizations build visibility, trust, and influence. As the founder of a boutique management consultancy, I've advised Fortune 500 companies, start-ups, nonprofits, and graduate students on how to position themselves for growth.

Along the way, I've trained more than 10,000 professionals—from CEOs to freshly minted MBAs—in digital presence, thought leadership, and employee advocacy. My work has earned industry recognition, including an Emmy Award for storytelling, and I've been invited to speak at conferences, teach at SMU's Cox School of Business, and consult for brands such as Dell, Nike, AT&T, and FedEx.

I love this work. I've seen it win multimillion-dollar deals, spark career-changing introductions, and open doors that seemed locked. I also know what it's like to start from scratch, to build credibility intentionally, one piece of content and one conversation at a time.

That's why I wrote this book, so you can do it, too. And, I want you to win!

Mindset

- While LinkedIn does not provide this statistic, I believe that less than 20 percent of LinkedIn users have a fully completed and marketable profile. (I've come to this conclusion after personally analyzing more than 10,000 LinkedIn profiles and developing my proprietary LinkedIn Scorecard, which is included later in this book.)
- In the Preface, I discussed where we are spending time on social media, and LinkedIn was at the bottom. Did you know:
    - There are 15 times more articles on LinkedIn than job postings? This means that conversations related to your industry, interests, and career are available for you to join at any time.
- There's a saying that I like: You can *spend* time on social media, or you can *invest* time on social media. The goal is to show you how investing a little bit of time strategically and intentionally is good for your career.
- At a high level, think of *investing* time as strategic and intentional time spent on platforms such as LinkedIn, where you add value to your connections and audiences by posting good stuff, sharing your unique perspective and point of view, and engaging with your network. This is a huge opportunity for you:
    - Less than 30 percent are consistently on the platform (posting and engaging).

- Less than 5 percent have a content strategy.

Strategic Effects

In each chapter, I will continue to draw back on the Strategic Effects framework I introduced you to in the Preface:

Observe – Orient – Analyze – Act – Repeat

This is how I've approached every business problem, brand challenge, and transformation project for the past 30-plus years. It applies just as well to your online reputation as it does to corporate strategy.

In this Introduction, you've already seen the first two stages in action.

- *Observe*: Recognize how today's first impressions happen online and how your digital footprint is shaping perceptions, often before you realize it.
- *Orient:* Understand the new landscape of trust and credibility. The rules haven't changed, but the scale has.

As we move into the next chapters, we'll go deeper into the remaining stages:

- *Analyze* how your current online presence performs.
- *Act* by building and sharing proof of your expertise.
- *Repeat* so you can learn from every interaction to stay relevant and visible.

Your reputation is no longer static. It evolves at the speed of search, so your approach and strategy need to evolve as well.

Key Takeaways / Recap

- Your digital reputation precedes you.
- You are your greatest asset. Invest accordingly and opportunities will find you!

- Executive 1 (Joseph) disqualified (or dis-validated) himself by not having a digital presence.
- Invest your time intentionally on social media versus mindlessly spending your time on platforms.
- I want you to win!

QR Code

CHAPTER 1
Origin Stories

Why Origin Stories Matter

Creating the "How You Got Here" That Makes People Want to Connect.

Every great hero, company, and career has an origin story. It's the "How did you get here?" moment that makes people lean in. When developed and delivered in the right way, it's what makes you interesting.

Most of us have not thought about origin stories as part of our careers. We are more used to seeing them in movies. Below are two of my favorite origin stories:

- Superman—Sent from a dying planet, raised in Kansas, searching for purpose.
- Iron Man—Billionaire weapons maker nearly dies, redefines himself as a force for good.

These origin stories connect us to heroes by making them relatable, despite their extraordinary abilities. They showcase vulnerability, personal struggles, and transformation—universal experiences that resonate with audiences.

Both of these stories remind us that challenges shape who we become, making these characters more than just icons. They become reflections of our own struggles, choices, and aspirations.

We relate to them because they're *human*. (Yes, technically Clark Kent is not human, but you get the gist.) The stories reveal qualities that build connection: vulnerability, transformation, and purpose.

Your career probably won't involve saving Metropolis or building a flying suit. But your origin story can still make people want to do business with you, hire you, or champion you.

Origin Stories in Business

An origin story explains the beginning of something, whether it's a person, a brand, a movement, or even an idea. It's the narrative that answers the foundational question: "How did this come to be?" These stories ground us in history, provide context, and create a framework for understanding.

In regards to business origin stories, one of the most common ones is, *This company started in a garage.* This list includes the following:

- Hewlett-Packard (HP)—Bill Hewlett and Dave Packard launched their company in a one-car garage in Palo Alto in 1939.
- Apple—Steve Jobs and Steve Wozniak founded Apple in the Los Altos garage of Jobs's parents in 1976.
- Google—In 1998, Google was started in a rented garage in Menlo Park by Stanford students Larry Page and Sergey Brin.
- Amazon—Jeff Bezos began Amazon as an online bookstore in his Bellevue, Washington, garage in 1994.
- Microsoft—Bill Gates and Paul Allen started their company from a garage in Albuquerque, where they developed their first BASIC interpreter.

There are other stories outside tech but still "garage born."

- Disney—Walt Disney and his brother started their animation business in their uncle's garage in Kansas City in the early 1920s.
- Matte—Elliot and Ruth Handler cofounded Mattel in a Los Angeles garage in 1945, originally making picture frame parts and later toys.
- In-N-Out Burger—While not a business run full-time from a garage, the fast-food chain's founder, Harry Snyder, invented the two-way drive-thru speaker system in his garage in 1948.

The "garage origin story" resonates because it conveys the following:

- Resourcefulness—Starting with minimal infrastructure; scrappy.
- Independences—Operating outside traditional corporate settings.
- Authenticitys—A compelling narrative that adds gravitas to a brand.
- Lack of perfect conditionss—Implying possibility for others.

These stories tap into the entrepreneurial mythos of transforming humble tools, a strong idea, and passion into something legendary.

Humans are naturally drawn to origin stories. They are an integral part of the human experience, passed down through generations.

> Origin stories became part of my professional journey and are now one of my mantras: Understand the why. I took this point of view when I began my first post-MBA job walking into that tech company. I didn't want to be one of those MBA-know-it-alls. Instead, I invested heavily in understanding the technology platforms, the history of how it became what it was when I started, how it actually worked, and how to use it. That put me in a position to lead the key piece of the business that generated more than a billion dollars annually.

Key Takeaway

Too many times, we are afraid that we have to be super "buttoned up" on LinkedIn—that we have to be perfect, polished, and nothing but professional. This is a mistake.

Instead, you should focus on being human, someone people can relate to and with whom they can connect.

I call this *human to human (H2H)*, and it's a mindset that pushes us beyond the limitations of business when we think only in terms of business to business (B2B) or business to consumer (B2C).

You need to be human on LinkedIn. People need to be able to relate to you.

Digital Validation^{TM} Origin Story #1: My Origin Story

TL;DR

Let's assume that Joseph, from Part 1 of The Tale of Two Executives, was the first origin story of this book. Now I want to share one of mine.

To cut a long story short, I was helping a friend start a video production company when social media was just becoming mainstream. It was the early days, much like the "Wild West days" of the dot com era.

We were creating content for two large brands, sharing our lessons learned along the way and integrating online, offline, and legacy media (TV) when a headhunter reached out to me.

I wasn't looking for a job and didn't have an updated resume. The headhunter discovered me because I was sharing things from both my day job (management consulting work) and the things we were learning from my friend's start-up.

The headhunter had a special, unadvertised pet-project for Michael Dell and thought I was a great fit. He thought this because I was active, visible, and adding value in what I was doing online.

This activity made me visible and interesting to a recruiter who was trying to fill an unadvertised position.

The Longer Story

There I was, busy with life: working for one of the world's largest and most prestigious management consulting firms, juggling family life that included two small kids and moonlighting—helping a friend get his video production company up and running.

As part of his business launch, we were testing new technology platforms called social media. You might recognize some of the names: Facebook, YouTube, and Twitter were the big three at the time. Remember that YouTube launched in December 2005. Facebook opened up to non-college students (over age 13) in September 2006. And Twitter launched in March 2006.

The moonlighting job was interesting. It was cutting edge, just like the dot com days when I managed a $1 billion e-commerce product line and later helped set up many of the retail systems that we take for granted today, the systems that enable us to see retailer inventory online or purchase online and return in store. I loved helping my friend because I was learning and having fun at the same time.

For the video production company, we wound up landing Anheuser-Busch and Maui Jim sunglasses as clients. Additionally, we built a 935,000-plus following online TV program (on the now defunct Google Hangouts) and won an Emmy in 2009 as part of our work.

So there I was, minding my own business with everything I just described from above when the phone rings.

Hello?

Is this Knox? My name is John Smith, and I'm an executive recruiter working on a project for Michael Dell. [His real name was not John Smith.]

Yes, speaking.

Michael likes what you are doing.

He does? I guess that's good. What specifically does he like? [I had no idea what he was talking about. Like I said, I was busy, minding my own business—that is, not looking for a job.]

I hear John chuckle.

Knox, do you have a few minutes to chat?

Yes, you caught me at a good time.

It was Friday afternoon, when, in a consultant's life, 9 times out of 10 you were done for the week minus the administrative work like expense reports.

I see that you're currently employed with Infosys and that you've done some really great work over the years with Sabre, Nokia, and Chevron.

[This was all on my LinkedIn profile. My resume was at least three years old because that's how long I had been at Infosys. That's the only place I thought John could have found this information—on LinkedIn.]

But what caught Michael's eye is the amount of quality work you've been doing with social media.

Thank you. What specifically would you like to know?

We went on to talk for more than an hour and a half. John shared the story of Dell Hell and how they were using tools such as Radian 6 to listen in on conversations taking place on social media, looking for customers in distress, so they could better serve them. Dell was looking for someone to productize this work and sell it through their consulting practice, all things that aligned with my career at the time. In the end, this led to a six-figure project for me.

Dell Summary

An unadvertised, well-paying consulting opportunity landed in my lap out of nowhere because I had been sharing valuable information on LinkedIn and other social media platforms. A headhunter had discovered me because I had been *sharing good stuff*, an early and now forgotten social media mantra.

Knox Tip: Opportunities don't always knock. Sometimes they start with someone Googling you.

The Professional Origin Story

I bet you've never framed your career as an origin story. But you should!

Another of my mantras is this: *Facts tell; stories sell.*

Remember, humans are naturally drawn to origin stories. They are an integral part of the human experience, passed down through generations. Stories are sticky.

An origin story explains the beginning of something, whether it's a person, a brand, a movement, or even an idea. These stories ground us in history, provide context, and create a framework for understanding.

Origin stories are narratives that answer: "How did this come to be?" When told well, it does this following:

1. Establishes identity—Shows who you are at your core
2. Builds connection—Creates an emotional bond
3. Creates meaning—Anchors your purpose and values
4. Sets the stage—Helps people understand your current path

Statistics

- People remember stories 22 times more than facts alone
- Stanford's Chip Heath discovered: 63 percent recalled stories, but only 5 percent remembered facts after just 10 minutes

Origin Story #2: Meet David (Part 2 of The Tale of Two Executives)

Let's turn to the story of another VP of sales, David. Like Joseph, David worked for a high-tech company and had just switched product lines that he was selling.

One morning over coffee, I asked David: "How will you let the market know you're now the go-to resource for Product B?" (instead of Product A).

He hadn't thought about it.

So we whiteboarded a plan:

- Optimize his team's LinkedIn profiles.
- Show up at conferences.
- Share value-driven content.
- Leverage existing company content.
- Amplify the team's individual posts.
- Be visible where the conversations were happening.

Within eight weeks, the team had a rhythm and a reputation. Then David received an unexpected call from a former client:

> *"David, I happened to see that you are now selling Product B. We were about to send an RFP [Request for Proposal] for Product B, so I wanted to make sure we reconnected."*

For those of you who have not experienced an RFP, it's a marathon, not a sprint.

A company announces that it's looking for a product or service, and vendors line up to respond. Each vendor answers hundreds of detailed questions about their offering and the services tied to it. Gathering the required information and submitting those responses can take months.

Once the paperwork has been submitted, the purchasing company narrows the list to three or four finalists. Those finalists are then invited to conduct on-site demos and presentations, adding another three to four months to the process.

By the time a decision is made, a year has often passed. Then comes contract negotiations and installations, which can easily push the timeline to 15 months or more.

The former client went on to say, "We have a solid relationship. You guys are clearly a leader in the space. If you guarantee me a great price, I can convince my leadership to skip the RFP ..."

That conversation became a $5 million sale that closed in under four months.

Existential Moments

Sometimes, origin stories begin when you stop mid-stride and ask: "How did I get here?"

This always reminds me of the Talking Heads song "Once in a Lifetime," as it nails this sentiment. Here is a snapshot of those lyrics:

> *And you may find yourself in another part of the world*
>
> *And you may find yourself behind the wheel of a large automobile*
>
> *And you may find yourself in a beautiful house, with a beautiful wife*
>
> *And you may ask yourself, "Well, how did I get here?"*

Life can pull you along on autopilot—career, family, responsibilities, etc.—until something forces you to pause.

Like sailing, your career rarely moves in a straight line. Wind shifts. Currents change. So you constantly tack, that is, assess where you are (observe), analyze, and adjust the sails to get back on course to your destination.

The point is that unless we are *intentional*, life can steer us off course from that straight-line trajectory we expect of always moving upward.

Strategic Effects

Throughout our careers we need to stop and perform a current state assessment, even when things are going well. We can employ *Strategic Effects*, where we assess (*observe* and *orient*), analyze, and act (aka, check our coordinates and the conditions, then tack), so we can right our course.

Life will inevitably give us these unrequested moments. Some of mine have included a layoff, a divorce, caring for my parents at the end of their lives, a business partner's embezzling, and even lawsuits.

How will you be best prepared?

Reflection Prompt

What were your "tacking moments," times you intentionally needed to adjust your speed, sails, and direction to stay on course?

Knox POV:

"Being truly seen builds trust. Trust accelerates deals."

Summary of Joseph vs. David: The Tale of Two Executives

JOSEPH	DAVID
Not Intentional	Intentional
No Strategy	Strategic
Invisible Online	Strong Digital Footprint
No Thought Leadership	Industry Thought Leader
Dis-validated Himself	Created Opportunities

Combining the stories of Joseph and David to create The Tale of Two Executives shows us the power of being intentional and visible in our careers.

Be Interesting, Not a Blowhard

David's success wasn't because he talked about himself nonstop. Instead, he added value by sharing insights, supporting his team's posts, and showing up where it mattered.

On LinkedIn, the same principle applies. The most interesting people are the ones shining the light on others, not just themselves. They engage in conversations. They add insights on other people's posts. They do not constantly talk about themselves and very rarely brag. They are interested in other people. They ask questions. They drive conversations and connections.

As Dale Carnegie said, "You can make more friends in two months by becoming interested in other people than you can in two years by trying to get people interested in you."

This is why I do not promote personal brands. You will hear me say this multiple times throughout this book. Personal brands are about individuals. They are rarely about adding value and mostly, if not always, take on a look-at-me mentality.

At best, from a marketing perspective personal brands *can* drive awareness, which is limited to the top of the sales funnel. In order to drive consideration and purchase, you must build credibility, trust, and connection—all things achieved when you focus on *professional* branding. More on this in Chapter 3.

Outside Perspective

In his book *Building a Storybrand*, Donald Miller states:

> *"Our brains are hardwired for story. If you confuse, you'll lose. If you clarify your story, you'll connect."*

This underscores why telling your own origin story matters. Miller continues:

> *"In every story, the character wants something and encounters obstacles to get it. Your story is no different. Show the struggle. It's what makes you human and relatable."*

As we create our origin stories, we must recognize that our imperfections and struggles are what make us human and relatable and help people connect with us. Too many times, we are focused on the transaction (closing the sale or landing the job) instead of building and nurturing a relationship.

Case Study: You Never Know Who Might Become Your Client

With every client I've had, I focus on getting to know people and building relationships. I tell my MBA students to focus on the relationship, not the title.

What do I mean by this? I can think of at least five people who worked at one of my client companies and then left to take on new roles at different companies. While they were at my client company, they had at least one of the following: no headcount or direct reports, no budget, or no authority to make purchasing decisions.

However, when they changed roles or companies, they often wound up having budgets, headcount, and decision-making authority. Because we had built relationships—and dare I say friendships—over the years, I had become a trusted advisor. And, unbeknownst to me, when they made their career changes, they wound up needing my services and called me.

Final Word on Origin Stories

The best origin stories are not polished; they are human. They are not highlight reels. They are moments of uncertainty, mistakes, pivots, and quiet realizations. They make us real to people with whom we want to connect.

On platforms like LinkedIn, we are trained to lead with credentials, titles, and perfectly staged wins, but that's not what creates trust. What connects us is the messy middle, the moments when we were unsure and had to continue going forward while trying to figure it out.

As Patrick Lencioni writes in *Getting Naked:*

"Vulnerability is not a weakness; it's the quickest path to building trust."

I know this title sounds scandalous, but I promise it's a business book that uses storytelling to show how vulnerability isn't just human but a competitive advantage in building trust with clients. Your origin story should not be seen as an opportunity to show perfection. It should be about giving people something to hold onto, something they can see in themselves.

And here's a twist:Your story isn't really about *you*. It's about showing others what's possible for *them*.

> *"Some of my most meaningful opportunities didn't come from the perfect story; they came from the honest ones."*
>
> —Knox

Statistics

- Profiles with a compelling "About" section get 27 times more views.
- 92 percent of consumers say they trust leaders who are visible and authentic online.

Exercise: Draft Your Origin Story

Capture the first things that come to mind.

1. Catalyst—What sparked a change or decision in your career?
2. Struggle—What challenge did you face?
3. Transformation—How did you grow or overcome it?
4. Purpose—What drives you today because of that moment?
5. Lesson—If you had one takeaway to share, what is it?

Origin Stories for Small Businesses

Every business has a story: how it came to be, how it grew, or how it survived. A well-crafted origin story does more than inform. It builds credibility, creates emotional connection, and makes your business memorable.

Your story doesn't need to start in a garage! It just needs to be *real*: Where did you start? What challenges did you face? What inspired you to build something different?

When you tell that story with clarity, customers will buy into *you*.

Example:

A corporate employee burns out from the nine-to-five grind and decides to start their own consulting business, driven by a desire for freedom and a passion for helping others succeed.

Why Origin Stories Matter in Business—Human to Human (H2H)

A well-crafted origin story does more than entertain; it builds credibility, humanizes your brand, and creates emotional engagement. It's not just about what you do, but why you do it.

People want to do business with people they know and trust. That's why I focus less on B2B or B2C and more on H2H: human to human.

Your origin story is the bridge that makes you relatable, trustworthy, and memorable.

The power of knowing, owning, and sharing your *origin* story is important in establishing how you show up and who connects with you.

Outside Perspective

Simon Sinek, author of *Start with Why*, built a global movement around a simple idea:

"People don't buy what you do; they buy why you do it."

That's exactly what an origin story does. It reveals the *why* behind your work, the spark that makes your professional journey memorable, relatable, and believable.

Titles change. Resumes evolve. Your why is what makes people lean in. It's what transforms a LinkedIn profile from a list of jobs into a story worth following.

Key Takeaway

Your why is not fluff. It's your foundation.

Summary

In our non-analog (aka digital) society, opportunity doesn't knock; it searches. Your origin story is your chance to make sure opportunities find you.

Whether you're a professional or small business owner, your story is more than a resume or a brand statement. It is a foundation of trust. It's how people will remember you and why they will choose to work with you.

QR Code

CHAPTER 2
You Will Be Googled

Have you ever Googled yourself? Seriously, have you? Googling yourself used to be a vanity metric or activity, but it is something you should do. (And I hope you followed the QR Code in the Preface and did the exercise!)

Statistic

- 8.5 billion name searches are conducted on Google every day.

Let that sink in: 8.5 billion! Recruiters, hiring managers, potential clients—and if you're single, potential dates—are looking you up and forming opinions about you before you ever step into a room with them or hop on a Zoom call.

Who else Googles you?

This list includes journalists and writers, legal professionals, consumers or customers, and family members.

For our discussion purposes, we will keep it confined to our careers.

But the real question is this: Are you in control of what they find?

History Lesson: The Impact of Search Engines

In the mid-to-late 1990s, the Internet started spreading into more homes due to dial-up connections like AOL and CompuServe. Google first launched in September 1998. (Yes, when my kids were in elementary school, I reminded them that I am older than Google!) In 2002 Google overtook Yahoo! Search as the most-used search engine, and in 2006 Google became the undisputed #1 search engine in the world.

Search engines didn't just change technology; they changed *us*. They reshaped how we think, how we learn, and how we judge one another.

Take something as simple as not knowing. Not long ago saying, "I don't know" was common. When you didn't know something, such as when discussing trivia or a sports statistic with friends, you would need to do research to find the answer. We either checked an encyclopedia or simply lived with the mystery. Today, those three words, *I don't know*, are almost extinct. The moment we don't know something, we Google it.

My friends have a standard response when someone shrugs off a question: *"GTS! [Google That Shit]."*

This is more than a convenience. Psychologists call it *The Google Effect*: Instead of remembering facts, we now remember where to find them. Think about phone numbers. As a kid, I could rattle them off for dozens of people: my friends, family, and even our local pizza place. Today? I barely know my own kids' numbers. We've outsourced memory to the cloud or our phones.

This shift has created what I call a culture of instant validation. In the pre-Internet era, finding an answer required effort. You went to the library, asked an expert, or dug through reference books. Now, we expect answers immediately. If a web page takes more than three seconds to load, most people click away.

Recruiters operate the same way: They expect your digital footprint to be accessible instantly, with no friction. If it's not, they move on.

Statistics

- Recruiters spend an average of six seconds scanning a resume.
- Goldfish have an attention span of eight seconds.
- Less than 1 percent of users click past the first page of search results.

Another consequence is what some call the *page two graveyard*. There's an old marketing joke that the best place to hide a dead body is on page two of Google search results. And it's true: Less than 1 percent of users ever click past the first page of search results. In other words, if your validation doesn't show up in those first 10 results, it might as well not exist at all.

And then there's the problem of expertise. In the past, credibility was centralized with professors, scientists, and authors. You trusted an encyclopedia because experts had written and vetted it. Today, anyone with a website can be a self-professed "expert."

Additionally, Google rewards the most optimized content, not necessarily the most accurate. Search "best diet for weight loss" and you'll get thousands of confident answers, many from people with no formal training. That makes it even more important that *you* show up online as a clear, consistent authority in your domain of expertise (aka, your career).

Finally, there's the permanence factor. In the newspaper era, a bad story eventually faded. Yesterday's controversy ended up on page 12 and was forgotten. Not anymore. Every comment, tweet, and photo lives online with no expiration date.

Recruiters will reject candidates based on what they find online, even if it's from years earlier. Your digital footprint doesn't just precede you; it follows you.

All of this brings us back to the central truth of this chapter: You will be Googled.

And when you are, people won't just be looking for you; they'll be looking for validation of who you are. What they see will shape whether they trust you, hire you, or dismiss you.

The First Time I Googled Myself

I had never Googled myself until I worked for Dell, but we were encouraged to do it as part of the social media training certification programs we developed. The first time I ran a search on my own name, I didn't just find myself, which was on page three of Google results. I found more people named Keith Knox (instead of Knox Keith).

Some were interesting: the professional baseball and rugby players, as well as the race car driver. Others were impressive: the minister, musician, and executives. But the one that stood out the most? That was Keith Knox, the Los Angeles County tax assessor and collector. Every year I am certain that name was cursed as those nine million residents wrote checks for their property taxes!

The problem wasn't that there were other Keith Knoxes. The real issue was that I wasn't owning my narrative. Anyone searching for me had to wade through pages of unrelated results. That's when I realized something important: If I don't control my story, someone else will. And if no one does, I become invisible.

Remembering The Tale of Two Executives

Previously we learned the stories of Joseph and David, two executives with two completely different approaches to building their own Digital

Validation™. Joseph chose to do nothing and lost a multi-million-dollar deal because of it.

David was intentional with his approach and closed a $5 million deal, skipping the lengthy sales lead time.

Joseph was invisible. David was undeniable. The difference? Digital Validation™.

Validated or Dis-validated? Your Choice

Most professionals do not realize that they are digitally disqualifying themselves every day by being inactive on LinkedIn or worse, by having only partially completed and out-of-date profiles.

Case Study: Open To Work

Most people assume that saying "open to work" on LinkedIn is enough to be found on LinkedIn. It isn't.

A friend of mine recently found a candidate who was perfect for a $100K role. When he tried to reach out to her, there was no email, phone number, or activity on her profile.

I even reached out to the seven mutual connections I had with her to help my friend. No one knew how to reach her.

This is the digital equivalent of sending out a resume with no contact information. While no one sends out a resume without contact information, the majority of people on LinkedIn do not provide an email address, yet alone a phone number. Don't let this be you!

Side note: Some of this can be attributed to privacy settings or the default of LinkedIn limiting contact information to only first-degree connections. Regardless, you need to show an email address. In addition, I recommend you include your contact info in your About section.

The lesson is simple: If you want opportunities to find you, make yourself reachable. Add your email and phone under Contact Info. Enable InMail. Show up regularly. In today's job market, being invisible online means being out of the running.

Statistics

- Only 16 percent of LinkedIn users in the US log in daily.
- People check their email more than 15 times per day.

Why It Matters

Recruiters don't have time to track you down. (Remember their six seconds of scanning a resume?) If they can't reach you quickly, they'll move on.

Get in the habit of logging into LinkedIn multiple times each day!

Digital Footprints—What They Really Are

In the Preface, you were introduced to the term *digital footprints*. You may immediately think of your LinkedIn profile or maybe your Instagram account, but your digital footprint is far bigger than that. It's everything connected to your name online.

Some of it you control. Some of it you don't.

There are two kinds of footprints:

- Active footprint: This is the content you intentionally create: your LinkedIn posts, your About section, the blog you wrote last year, your Tweets, and even the profile picture you chose.
- Passive footprint: This is the content created by others that is left behind: that industry conference agenda PDF still floating around with your old job title, a random tag on Facebook from five years ago, or a review you left on Yelp that still shows up in search.

Here's the reality: recruiters, clients, hiring managers, and your HR department don't care which ones were active and which ones were passive; they see both. And that's all part of the puzzle they piece together about you.

Knox POV:

> *"You already have a digital footprint, whether you like it or not. The only question is whether it's intentional or accidental."*

Exercise

In the Preface you were prompted to Google yourself. Let's review that.

1. List the sources that show up.

   For me this list includes my blog, my website, Instagram, my company website, Pinterest, Twitter (I still can't call it "X"), LinkedIn, Facebook, WordPress, Flickr, and a former employer.

   What surprised you? Did anything show up that you'd forgotten about?

2. Separate active from passive.

   Which of those sites do you actively control (e.g., your blog, LinkedIn, company site)? And which do you not control (e.g., public directories, old employer pages, mentions in other people's content)?

   Remember: Both shape your reputation, but only one is in your hands. Where are your opportunities to control your narrative?

3. Identify the topics.

   What themes appear when someone Googles you? For me, the results were largely business-related: *Digital Validation, Strategic Effects,* and *consulting,* all of which are intentional and strategic. But there were also traces of personal content that popped up in social feeds.

   I control the content about me on those social feeds, and so should you about yourself. My social content helps humanize me, showing small glimpses of my personal life and the things I enjoy. This includes travel, food, and the outdoors.

4. Decide what you want to change.

   This is the most important step. You may find results that are outdated, inconsistent, or irrelevant. You may also notice areas where you need more visibility. Being intentional means shaping the narrative. For me, even my Instagram matters. The travel, food, and outdoor posts I share are carefully curated, polished glimpses into my life. They are not oversharing; they are controlled, human touches that help people relate to and connect with me.

   There is no action to take right now. We will cover this in detail starting in Chapter 8. For right now, you need to start thinking in these terms.

The Stakes of Being Googled

Let's take a moment and emphasize the one-two punch that is taking place:

- Punch number one: Surveys show that more than 90 percent of recruiters use LinkedIn to *find* candidates.
- Punch number two: 70 percent of those same recruiters will Google your name to *validate* what they see.

Think of it this way: You control what you put out there, and you choose whether you do this or not. (Think Joseph vs. David.) You cannot get hired for a position if people cannot see you. Even if they can see you, they will try to *validate* your credibility.

Additionally, more than half of employers (54 percent) have eliminated a candidate because of what they found online. Not because of a bad interview. Not because the person wasn't qualified. But because the digital footprint raised questions.

That's the power—and danger—of search.

"Your social posts aren't just for your followers. They're part of your digital footprints and the Google validation process."

—Knox

We saw this with Joseph in The Tale of Two Executives case study, where Joseph and his company were eliminated from winning the deal because Joseph's digital footprint (or lack thereof) raised a red flag to the purchasing Department in its decision-making process.

By contrast, David, Executive 2, shared articles about his product line. He engaged with people by commenting on other people's posts and posts from industry events. David became visible around his subject matter expertise through strategic and intentional posts.

David proved the value of a strong, consistent, professional, and intentional digital footprint.

Building a Validating Footprint

How do you make sure your footprint validates rather than disqualifies you? I use a simple framework:

1. *Consistency*

   Your name, image, title, and story should line up across every platform. If you're a VP of sales on LinkedIn but a "Sales Ninja" on Twitter, you've created a credibility gap. Same goes for using a consistent headshot.

2. *Authority + Thought Leadership*

   Share content that shows what you know and that adds-value. Not fluff. Not buzzwords. Substance. A strong footprint doesn't just say you're an expert; it proves it. (*It's the power of show, don't tell.)*

3. *Controlled Humanizing Content*

People want to know you're human. Add one or two personal interests and one charitable cause. (I talk about tacos, photography, and travel.) But keep it curated. This is the difference between connection and oversharing. More on this in Chapter 9.

4. *Accessibility*

   Make it easy for people to reach you. Your contact information should not be buried or missing. If you're open to work, make it frictionless for someone to send you an email or schedule a call. And then login in regularly to LinkedIn. Doing so will automatically jet you into the top 16 percent of LinkedIn users.

Rule of Seven in Marketing

We live in a visually bombarding society. We are always connected, always in front of a screen. One leading social media company that I've worked with states that it now takes seeing an image 17 times before our brain recognizes that it has seen that image before.

While I have not been able to confirm that number, let's fall back to the rule of seven in marketing. This rule suggests that you need to see something *seven times* before the message really sinks in.

Throughout this book, you may see me repeat things. Some people may roll their eyes at this. I'm thinking of my kids when they were teenagers: *Dad, you've already told me that* [with the eyeroll]. So there is a method behind this, and it's not because I think that you're not listening to me! Lol.

Case Study: Building Your LinkedIn Presence

I have seen the shift of moving from an *invisible* presence to a *visible* presence firsthand. A mid-level executive I worked with years ago had almost no digital footprint outside of a bare-bones LinkedIn profile. After she went through these steps—optimizing her profile, posting things of value consistently, engaging with other people's posts, and showing her personality through a cause she cared about—her online presence started to mirror the professional reputation she already had offline. Within six months, she was recruited into a bigger role at a Fortune 500 company.

That's Digital Validation™ in action.

Outside Perspective

"When I see someone with a skimpy LinkedIn profile—no banner image, maybe a photo, not much detail—I think they are one-dimensional, maybe even antisocial. Either they don't know they should be visible, or they just don't care. And in today's world, that says something whether they intend it to or not."

—Karen Imes, Marketing Expert

Karen's perspective underscores that you will be evaluated, if not judged, by *how* you show up online. Are you intentional and strategic? Are you doing the bare minimum? Or, are you invisible like Joseph from The Tale of Two Executives?

Continuing with Karen, the corollary is also true: "*When I see someone with a complete, active profile, I assume they enjoy their work and aren't afraid to share their thoughts. It tells me they're confident enough to be seen.*"

Which one do you want to be?

Key Takeaways

Your presence is digitally evaluated before you ever enter the room.

- You will be Googled.
- Recruiters, clients, and hiring managers form opinions before they even meet you.
- Search visibility determines whether you're considered at all.
- Be on page one or be invisible.
- Less than 1 percent of people click past the first page of search results.
- Absence is still information—and it's rarely neutral.
- Silence = disqualification.
- More than 54 percent of employers have rejected candidates based on what they find, or don't find, online.

What you don't shape will still shape you.

- Own your own footprint.
- Active content builds credibility. Passive content still shapes perception. Control what you can.

Opportunity dies when friction exists.

- Be easy to reach.
- A perfect candidate with no contact info is a missed opportunity.

Trust is built through repetition, not bursts.

- Show up consistently.
- Consistency builds trust. Inconsistency erodes it.

LinkedIn isn't a personality vacuum. Professional doesn't mean generic.

- Be human, intentionally.
- Curated personal content connects. Oversharing repels.

Intention determines what you're known for.

- Consider validation vs. dis-validation.
- An intentional footprint builds clear professional association. Ambiguity can cost future opportunities.

QR Code

CHAPTER 3
Personal Brand vs. Professional Brand

The Problem with Personal Branding

In the last decade, personal branding has become a buzzword in professional circles. Influencers, entrepreneurs, and executives have been told to "build their personal brand," but what does that really mean?

For most, personal branding is nothing more than vanity metrics:

- The number of followers you have.
- The amount of likes your posts receive.
- The illusion of perceived value rather than actual value.

But here's the hard truth: Personal branding, as it is commonly taught, is all about "me," not the audience or client. It's broadcasting, not engaging. It's about awareness, not about building trust, credibility, or relationships. When brands invest in so-called "influencers" with large personal brands, they often find that those influencers provide zero tangible value in driving meaningful engagement or action. In other words, supposed influencers and those focusing on personal brands are creating noise and not value.

This ties to a marketing problem as it relates to the sales funnel: Awareness alone is not enough.

Think about the traditional sales funnel:

1. Awareness—People know you exist.
2. Consideration— People start seeing you as credible.
3. Purchase/Action—People trust you enough to engage with your expertise.

Personal branding stops at awareness, the very top of the funnel. It can create visibility, but visibility without trust or credibility is meaningless.

Diving into the Problem with Personal Branding

I have a problem with personal branding. It has morphed into something it wasn't supposed to be, yet there is still a lot of focus on the term. Instead, we should pivot and focus more on professional branding.

The concept of a personal brand became mainstream in 1997 when Tom Peters wrote a *Fast Company* article titled "The Brand Called You." In it

Peters argued that, "We are CEOs of our own companies: Me, Inc." And, at the time, this was associated more with thinking and acting like your own publicist. And the concept was probably in its most pure form at that time.

When social media first hit the scene (think 2005–2010), suddenly everyone had their own media platform. LinkedIn (2003), Facebook (2004), Twitter (2006), and Instagram (2010) gave everyone tools to share their stories and their opinions. The adage "15 minutes of fame" was thrown to the wayside, and now the spotlight was no longer just reserved for celebrities; it was up for grabs for anyone who could generate the attention.

As social media matured, the loudest and most visible voices appeared to gain traction, even if they were not the most qualified voices.

As people started attracting audiences, they did become CEOs of their own company: Me, Inc. And in the process, credentials and experience were replaced with follower count (real or purchased). Value was replaced with "going viral," and expertise was replaced with aesthetics.

But all of this is shallow, as I will explain in the next few pages.

When we dive deeper into the sales funnel, we will see that personal branding has deviated from its original purpose. In 1997, Tom Peters framed it as *empowerment*. It was a call to action to do the following:

- Take control of your career.
- Don't rely on your employer, job title, or resume to define who you are or your value.

In short, the original personal branding was a way to help stand out in a crowded, competitive professional world. It was about the following:

- Owning your narrative.
- Differentiating yourself.
- Being proactive about your reputation.
- Marketing your strengths intentionally.

At the time, it was a powerful counterbalance to how so many of us from an older generation were raised to wait our turn and let our work speak for itself.

But here's the twist: The Internet and later social media amplified the concept to its extremes.

What began as a tool for career ownership and visibility morphed into a tool for attention.

The original intent was for you to shift your mindset to being more of a publicist for your career. It was strategic and professional. The modern version is more aesthetic, performative, and self-absorbed, with little to no value. Because personal branding does not focus on value, it has become more noise.

To me, personal branding is now shallow. There is no depth behind it. I'll share with you how I came to these conclusions in the rest of this chapter, as well as how we should be thinking about it.

> *"When you build for attention, you get noise. When you build for relationships, you get momentum. Attention may get you noticed. Trust is what keeps you respected."*
>
> —Ted Rubin, author: *Return on Relationship*

Why It Matters

Personal branding started as a way to take control of your career, not as a megaphone for vanity metrics. Somewhere along the way, the concept was hijacked by algorithms, aesthetics, and attention merchants.

Why does this matter? Because attention without trust doesn't convert.

In business and in life, people don't make decisions because someone is the loudest voice in the room. They make decisions because they trust the source. And trust isn't built by going viral; it's built through credibility, proof, and consistency over time.

This is why *professional* branding matters so much more than personal branding. Professional branding moves you beyond visibility into the territory of influence and action.

When your reputation precedes you in the right way, doors open faster. Your opportunities aren't limited to who you know; they're amplified by what people can find, see, and trust about you online.

Let's dive into some definitions.

Definitions

- *Publicists* manage visibility and reputation. Their job is to get you noticed, quoted, invited, featured, and remembered, but always in the right context.

  They focus on the following:

  - Crafting your narrative.
  - Pitching your expertise.
  - Securing interviews, guest spots, and speaking gigs.
  - Managing how you're perceived by the public.

  In short, a publicist doesn't just help you get seen; they help shape what people see.

  In his article, Tom Peters didn't just say, "Build a personal brand." He was telling us to act like our own publicist long before that became normal.

  At the time, that was radical. Today, it's a requirement, but it has to be the right kind of publicity. One that helps prove your credibility. One that helps you build trust with your audience. One that is consistently adding value over time.

- *Personal branding* is the act of promoting yourself—your personality, lifestyle, and opinions—as the product. It's designed to build your recognition and reach, often with the goal of becoming an *influencer*.

At its core, personal branding has become all about being known or famous. The goal is to attract followers, meaning grow your audience to build perceived authority in order to monetize attention.

In this process, you construct a curated image and are focused only on yourself and awareness. It is "me" focused, as in, "Look at me! Look at me! I'm important! You should listen to my opinions."

Personal branding has become repeatedly telling people that you are important.

- *Professional branding* is the act of positioning yourself based on expertise, credibility, consistency, and the value you deliver to others. It is less about being known and more about being relevant and trusted.

  At its core, professional branding is not about you. Instead, it is about the problem you solve, the perspectives you share, and the results you help create.

  The goal of professional branding is to consistently add value, and as a result of doing so over time, build trust. It is the driving factor that moves people and decisions through the sales funnel from awareness to consideration to purchase.

  Professional branding is proof of who you are, what you know, where you've been, and where you're going. It is not the personal hype that personal branding has become. It is not about follower count or attention seeking. It is about adding value.

  Let me repeat that for those in the back. Professional branding is about helping other people. It is about adding value consistently over time. In doing so, you become a credible resource that people trust and from whom they eventually consider purchasing products and services.

In the process of doing this, you never tell people that you are important. Instead, others determine that you are important because you have added value to your audiences consistently over time.

Interview with Alex Irvin, Public Relations Consultant

Question: *In your experience, what separates a public persona that is remembered versus one that is forgotten?*

Answer: *There is so much noise in every industry with people competing for attention and relevance. Widespread recognition won't happen overnight (and if it does, it's likely for a bad reason). Consistent engagement, meaningful replies, and nurturing actual relationships, even if it is in small steps, all build toward something memorable.*

Building a memorable persona requires the following:

1. Consistency
2. Dialogue
3. Authenticity
4. Uniqueness

Now let me introduce the sales funnel.

The Sales Funnel

My simplified sales funnel highlights three key areas or stages that marketing and sales professionals use to drive or convert a sale.

1. Awareness: The top of the funnel

This is when people first learn about you or your product. It's all about visibility: your name, face, or logo. Personal branding lives here. It is limited to this space only. Personal branding is all about broadcasting and saying, "Look at me! I am important!"

Goal of awareness: Get noticed.

2. Consideration: The middle of the funnel

This is where people ask: "Is this person or resource credible? Are they legitimate? Can they help me? Can I trust them?"

Professional branding starts to take over here. You are not just visible. You are credible because your content and your activities add value. It's because your digital footprint shows proof, and your reputation has built trust.

Goal of consideration: Establish credibility / Become a trusted resource.

3. Purchase (or Decision): The bottom of the funnel

Now people are ready to take action: hire you, refer you, invite you, promote you, or buy from you. Your consistent value over time has pulled them down or through the sales funnel.

Goal of purchase: Create conversion or commitment.

Putting It All Together

	PERSONAL BRANDING	PROFESSIONAL BRANDING
PRIMARY GOAL	Be seen, liked, followed	Be trusted, respected, referred
FOCUS	Promoting yourself as the product	Adding value
AUDIENCE APPEAL	"Look at me!"	"Here's how I can help you."
MOTIVATION	Influence, attention, audience growth	Impact, credibility, opportunity
CONTENT TYPE	Lifestyle, opinions, behind-the-scenes	Insights, results, thought leadership
FUNNEL FIT	Awareness only	Consideration → Action
TRUST LEVEL	Can feel curated or performative; fake	Built through consistency and value
RISKS	Vanity metrics, low ROI, short shelf life	Requires time, but builds long-term equity
BEST FOR	Aspiring influencers, creators, self-promotion	Consultants, leaders, service providers, job seekers

Outside Perspective

"Awareness can create visibility, but visibility without trust or credibility is meaningless."

—Amanda Russell, *The Influencer Code* (SXSW Interview)

Knox POV: Only professional branding makes a real impact on sales. Personal branding has become just more noise in an already crowded space.

"Invest in professional visibility, not just grabbing attention. When you do, you will build credibility that over time turns to trust. Trust is what converts."

Case Study: Celebrity Influencer

One of my manufacturing clients hired a big-time celebrity influencer. Personally, when I think of a celebrity, I think of a professional athlete, a musician, an actor, or a performer. Perhaps a politician or even some CEOs. This woman's claim to fame was a reality TV show and a high-profile divorce from a professional athlete.

She was hired for $1 million to show up to an event, have a few photos taken, make a short speech, and post a few pre-written things on social media.

The metrics that my client insisted we use were impressions, a vanity metric that has nothing to do with sales orders, landing pages, collecting sales leads, or qualified marketing leads. Impressions had nothing to do with driving people to our showrooms or to our distributors. There were no traceable coupon codes and tags to track web traffic. Nothing but impressions from the one-day event.

Needless to say, this "influencer" had zero pull in this particular industry. The client's marketing team, against our advice, thought they would naturally get a million-plus views (or impressions) simply because this supposed influencer had nearly five million followers.

The campaign was a disaster. We didn't even earn 10,000 impressions. All because they were focused on a personal brand instead of a professional brand.

Months later we were able to pivot the client to an influencer who had more professional credibility in their manufacturing niche. He wasn't as well known nationally, but had his own TV show, a strong social following, and a regional pull. We were able to design a real marketing campaign focused on leveraging his professional expertise and credibility that was strongly tied to our industry to increase true awareness, impact consideration, and drive sales by thinking beyond vanity metrics.

This gentleman cost less than 10 percent of the original influencer and was a thousand times more valuable. That's not an exaggeration. He added value to us, his network, and everyone he worked with throughout the campaign. He went above and beyond his contractual obligations because he was focused on his relationship with us and the relationships with his audiences. This was not just a business transaction as it had been with the million-dollar cost influencer.

As a result of this well-orchestrated campaign, our manufacturing client saw real, impactful results: increases in website traffic, distributor store traffic, and showroom visits. Most importantly, our client saw a 15 percent increase in quarterly sales from the region where we focused this campaign!

Summary of Case Study

- Are you star-struck, or are you focused on making an impact?
- Too much focus on awareness at the top of the sales funnel does not guarantee impacts on conversions.
- Instead of limiting yourself to top-of-funnel awareness, think in terms of what will help move your clients to consideration and purchase / conversion.

Statistics

The numbers back it up:

- 47 percent of employers are *less likely* to interview a candidate they cannot find online, underscoring the importance of being visible and credible on digital platforms.
- People with a fully completed LinkedIn profile are 40 times more likely to receive job opportunities through the platform

People Trust People, Especially Those at the Top

CEOs need a strong, professional brand, too.

A study found that when CEOs have a strong individual brand, their content generates nearly five times more engagement than their company's official channels.

That isn't just a marketing statistic. It's proof that trust flows through people, not logos.

Even at the highest levels of leadership, a professional brand matters. A CEO's digital footprint can humanize an organization, make strategy relatable, and turn corporate messages into conversations.

And if this principle holds true for a CEO, it's even more powerful for professionals building their own reputations.

Remember, people buy into people, long before they buy into a product, service, or brand.

Key Takeaways

Even if professional branding isn't yet a widely used term, how you are seen online, the content you share and the way you engage make a difference in how you're perceived and whether you are credible.

Knox POV:

Show, don't tell. Anyone can tell you anything online. They can *say* they're a great leader, strategist, or trusted advisor. But unless they show it, those claims don't carry much weight.

That's why professional branding isn't just about positioning; it's about proof. When you consistently share insights, stories, and results, you're offering evidence of your expertise. You're building a digital paper trail (or *digital footprint*) around value.

Later in this book, we'll talk more about how this approach doesn't just build trust; it also helps position you as a subject matter expert or thought leader in your field.

But it all starts with the mindset: *Show, don't tell.*

"Personal branding is about attention.
Professional branding is about trust."

Human to Human or H2H

People do not buy from faceless brands; they buy from people they know and trust. In fact, a staggering 92 percent of consumers trust recommendations from someone they know personally, far more than any other form of advertising.

This is why professional branding isn't just about claiming credibility; it's about providing evidence that earns trust. Later in this book, we'll explore how that credibility, shown over time, naturally elevates you into the role of a trusted subject matter expert or thought leader.

The Progression to Trust: From Control to Credibility

At AT&T, we often used a slide called the *progression to trust* to explain how credibility is built, not given. The slide shows how influence (or trust) moves from low-trust, high-control channels (like ads or websites) to high-trust, low-control relationships (like peer recommendations or personal referrals).

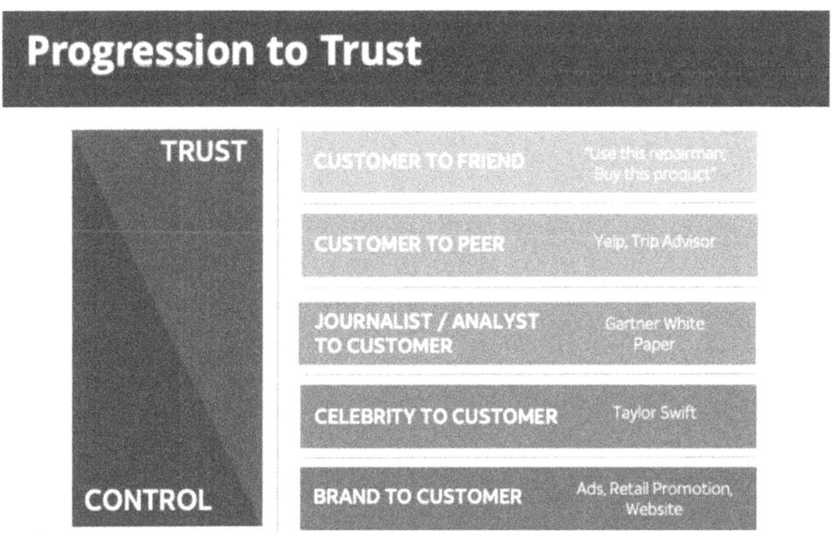

Let's break that down:

- When a brand tells you to buy something (via ads or retail promotions), you know that they are selling. That's the lowest trust tier and the highest form of control by the brand.
- A celebrity endorsement might get attention, but unless that celebrity has credibility in the category, it does not create confidence.
- Journalists or analysts, like those from Gartner or Forrester, bring more weight because they research before they recommend, but they may have been paid by the brand for publishing a positive piece.
- Peer reviews (Yelp, TripAdvisor, etc.) move the needle even more because we trust people like us.
- And finally, the highest form of trust comes from a friend or known expert, someone with shared context, credibility, and history. That's the human-to-human connection that drives decisions.

So, where do you fall on this trust spectrum?

If all you're doing is shouting into the void, posting content without adding value, you're stuck at the bottom level. But if you consistently deliver insights, results, and support, you move up the ladder. You become a trusted peer, the go-to resource, or the advisor. And that's the true return on investment (ROI) of professional branding.

Push vs. Pull Marketing

One of the most overlooked principles in how we present ourselves online is the difference between push and pull marketing. Push marketing is outbound. It interrupts. Think TV commercials, spam calls, or unsolicited email. This is marketing that is trying to grab attention primarily by broadcasting a message. These messages flow only in one direction; that is, push messages have no feedback. There is no dialogue. It is short-term, aggressive, and usually optimized for volume, hoping that it lands.

Pull marketing, on the other hand, is inbound. It attracts. It's built on value, credibility, and positioning.

Pull marketing doesn't beg for attention. It earns it. When done well, it's long-term, sustainable, and rooted in trust. It draws people in because you're offering insight, proof, and perspective. You have added value consistently over time.

Personal branding lives in the push category. It focuses on visibility for visibility's sake, highlighting lifestyle, aesthetics, and personality. It's built to catch attention, not necessarily to hold it. Most influencer-style personal brands are pushing content into the world with the hope it sticks, regardless of whether it helps anyone.

Professional branding, by contrast, is a pull strategy. It positions you as a trusted advisor, valuable resource, or subject matter expert. Instead of saying, "Look at me," you're saying, "Here's something useful for you." Your content becomes a magnet, not a megaphone. Over time, this is what moves someone from awareness to consideration to action. People don't feel sold to. Instead, they feel served. That's the foundation of trust. Lastly, professional branding should invite conversations, meaning that it is not one-sided or one-direction communication, like personal branding.

Personal branding does not leverage social media the right way. Social media is meant to be social or conversational. When social media is leveraged for only broadcasting messages, then it's just media, and the message becomes noise.

When you think about your own online presence, ask yourself this: Am I pushing my way into someone's feed, or pulling them into a deeper relationship? The strongest professional brands never shout. They attract.

Outside Perspective

In his book *Return on Relationship*, Ted Rubin reframes the equation: Reach gives you attention, but relationships give you lasting value. Value is the real, lasting gain that comes when trust, loyalty, and advocacy are at the core of how you show up online.

> *"ROR: Return on Relationship ... simply put, is the value that is accrued by a person or brand due to nurturing a relationship. ROI is simple $'s and cents. ROR is the value (both perceived and real) that will accrue over time through connection, trust, loyalty, recommendations, and sharing."*
>
> —Ted Rubin, *Return on Relationship*

Takeaways

- Personal branding is limited to awareness and broadcasting of messages. These are push marketing tactics.
- Professional branding focuses on others and adding value to them consistently over time. This generates trust and pull marketing, helping move people through the sales funnel.
- People do business with people. This is human to human or H2H.
- Show, don't Tell.

QR Code

CHAPTER 4
LinkedIn Is More than a Resume and Rolodex

What Is a Rolodex?

I recently saw a parent (probably my age, mid-50s) sit their teenage daughter down and interview her while filming. She told the daughter a series of terms that we grew up with to see if the daughter knew what they were. The terms included: Yellow Pages, dial-up, answering machine, beepers (pagers), VHS, Blockbuster, mixtape, long distance (dialing), phone cords, pay phones, and Rolodex. The daughter knew none of them! Absolutely zero! It made me want to research the gap between my parents' and my generations. But that's for another time.

For those of you too young to know, here's the definition for *Rolodex*:

> A rotating desktop file device used for storing business contact information on individual cards, organized alphabetically. Popular from the 1950s through the 1990s, the Rolodex was a staple of office culture and networking before the rise of digital contact management systems.

Before smartphones and LinkedIn, professionals kept their network in a spinning card file on their desk. The Rolodex held business cards or handwritten info, and the size of yours often said something about your status. It was your offline contact list before "contacts" went digital.

LinkedIn Should Be More Than Your Rolodex

Why am I mentioning this? It's because people loosely use LinkedIn, along with their cell phones and email accounts, as a Rolodex for their professional contacts.

And you should have a system for managing your professional contacts. If LinkedIn is that tool for you, it should not be the only thing LinkedIn does for you. Yes, LinkedIn can be a place for you to hold onto professional relationships, be they strong or weak. (Think acquaintance versus someone you recently met at a conference.) These are people who you do not know at a deeper level. You may not be contacting them regularly as you might with those in your phone or email contacts.

People will change jobs, which means their emails change, but you can still keep abreast of their professional endeavors through LinkedIn.

Now that everyone knows what a Rolodex is, let's jump into *why* LinkedIn should be more than a resume and Rolodex for you.

Why It Matters

LinkedIn isn't just a digital business card; it's your career storefront, reputation engine, and opportunity generator. If you treat it like a static file cabinet, it'll collect digital dust. If you treat it like a living, breathing network, it can create visibility, trust, and career momentum long before you need it.

Key Point 1: LinkedIn Is Not Your Resume. It's So Much More!

What do I mean by this? Let's start with what your resume (or CV) is: a one- to two-page page snapshot of some of the things you've done professionally. It's a fact sheet.

> *Knox Keith worked as director of The Princeton Review from 1994–1996. Here are three things he did there.*
>
> *Knox Keith graduated from The University of Texas at Austin in 1991. He earned a Bachelor of Arts in English Literature and minors in Spanish and Business. (Just another fact.)*

And, in some cases, a resume might include an objectives or goals statement.

That's it.

Resumes are static. That is, they do not move. They are snapshots of your past. They are not living things.

A resume's existence is very limiting. People only see it when you send it out when you are looking or applying for a job.

Your resume should therefore be viewed as "dead."

But LinkedIn is alive, especially if you are active on the platform, sharing good stuff, adding value to and engaging with your network.

Knox POV: Facts tell; stories sell.

If you are active on LinkedIn, then every day thousands of people in your network and outside your network have the opportunity to see you, learn about you, and engage with your thoughts. And yes, if you have an updated and optimized profile, they can view your career history.

But on LinkedIn, people can see your thoughts and learn about your personality and leadership styles. They cannot do this with a resume.

Let's look at it this way:

- A resume compresses you into bullets.
- LinkedIn expands you into a story.
- Your About section, featured content, recommendations, and activity feed give hiring managers, clients, or collaborators a deeper sense of your mindset, voice, and values. LinkedIn provides people with a three-dimensional view of you.
- LinkedIn shares more than just what you did. It can show how you think and how you work.

Another way to look at LinkedIn is as your career storefront. The starting point of how 95 percent of recruiters might discover you and learn more about you. Designed and used correctly, LinkedIn can generate leads for you!

LinkedIn should not be static like your resume. It should be the place where you share your experiences, make new connections, nurture existing relationships, and ultimately build influence.

Knox POV: What Influence Is (and Is Not)

Influence is not about being the loudest voice in the feed. It's about building trust, sharing value, and being visible in a way that aligns with your professional reputation.

Influence is earned through consistency and credibility—not virality.

Right now, if someone views your LinkedIn profile, what will they see? An abandoned storefront? A partially complete profile? No engagement? No thought leadership? No digital footprint, not even the bare minimum?

You own your career story, and LinkedIn has provided you with an awesome opportunity to share it. It's accessible 24/7. It is the place for you to be discovered and seen.

Keep in mind, much like staying in good physical shape, LinkedIn requires a commitment. It is not a place to "set it and forget it." And your fitness journey isn't over after just one trip to the gym. Perhaps you should think of LinkedIn like a farmer. Their job isn't done once the seeds are in the ground.

Planting is just the beginning. There's watering, weeding, protecting, monitoring the weather, fending off pests, and showing up every single day to check on growth.

A successful harvest doesn't come from intention alone; it comes from attention.

Your LinkedIn presence works the same way. Just setting up a nice profile and walking away doesn't build a reputation. You have to nurture it and tend to it. You have to show up regularly.

That means staying active, contributing to conversations, celebrating others, adding insights, and updating your presence as you grow.

The people who win on LinkedIn are not always the loudest; they're the ones who stay present and show up consistently.

So no, LinkedIn is not a "set it and forget it" tool. It's a garden. The more you care for it, the more it produces.

To make LinkedIn more than a resume, you have to *invest* your time on the platform. As opposed to other social media platforms where we tend to spend (or waste) our time. To make LinkedIn more than a snapshot of your professional journey, be prepared to dedicate time to it.

Knox POV: Ironically, more than 70 percent of people on LinkedIn have an incomplete profile.

"Want to stand out on LinkedIn? Fully optimize your profile, and you will immediately have an advantage over the majority of people."

Key Point 2: LinkedIn Is Not a Rolodex. It's So Much More!

To reap the full benefits of LinkedIn, it has to become more than a Rolodex for you.

A Rolodex is similar to the resume in that it is also static. A Rolodex is just a collection or repository of names and numbers and perhaps business names and job titles.

LinkedIn has much of the same information as a Rolodex, but it also shows you how you are connected. You can see your mutual connections, the job histories of your connections, and the activity (posts and comments) of your connections. More importantly, LinkedIn shows how you interact with others.

Comments, shares, posts, endorsements, featured content, and charitable associations all paint a picture of how you show up in the real world and how you operate in a community. Your digital footprint shows whether you're generous, insightful, collaborative, invisible, egotistical, and more.

By actively and consistently participating on LinkedIn, you are acting as your own publicist, crafting your professional narrative, and building and nurturing your professional community.

LinkedIn is your chance to show, don't tell! You can prove yourself before you ever walk into a room and craft your story by adding value to your network. This is how you build trust and a strong, consistent, and professional online presence. You can establish social proof for your career long before you ever hit the 'apply' button or send out a resume!

LinkedIn is the platform where your Digital Validation™ begins and lives. It is the platform where your online presence proves your professional reputation. When someone Googles your name, LinkedIn is a top contributor to where you rank.

And here's the risk: If your LinkedIn presence looks abandoned or incomplete and you are inconsistent or not engaged, that's exactly what you communicate to the world.

Knox POV: When I've held marketing leadership positions, I paid very little attention to someone's resume. I am more interested in how they showed up online. If you have a career in marketing and you cannot even do the bare minimum of marketing yourself on LinkedIn, then generally you are not going to work for me.

LinkedIn is your *professional online proof* that you are who you say you are.

Key Point 3: Content Is Your New Set of Credentials

Before we panic here about creating content, let's take a step back. I am not saying that you must create original content to be successful. Lord knows that when I first started experimenting with social media and blogs were becoming a big deal, I panicked. As busy as I was, I could not fathom having to write original content on a regular basis.

Let me also take a moment to introduce a concept that helps everyone. It's called *Crawl - Walk - Run.*

We will dig into this later, but here's an overview as it pertains to being active on LinkedIn:

- **Crawl:** Liking and reacting to content to start showing up.
- **Walk:** Commenting thoughtfully to build visibility.
- **Run:** Posting and leading conversations to shape your narrative.

We are all starting at different points in our LinkedIn / Digital Validation™ journey. As we move through this book, we will assess where we are: Beginners? Intermediate? Advanced? We will devise plans based on where we are. More on this later.

Back to content. I know what you're probably asking: *Hmmm, what do I share then if it's not an original article or blog?*

We all read. Hopefully we read things related to our careers and interests. In Chapter 10 (Build Your Content Framework) we will cover this in more depth. To start, we share what we are reading, what we are working on, or something of interest. We read a lot of things online, and most of those things have a 'share' button, where you can share it to your LinkedIn page.

Right now, I'm just giving you the concepts, but the motto is, *Share good stuff.* Share stuff that is interesting and insightful. Share stuff that is valuable to your network.

Out of grad school way back in 1998, life was very different. I was fortunate to have a great boss. One of the things he did was share good stuff, but it was way more difficult back then. It was analog!

For example, when Kevin found an interesting article in *Harvard Business Review*, he would photocopy it and stick it in an interoffice envelope with all of our names on it. We would have two weeks for the whole team to pass it around and read it. Then, once a month in a staff meeting, we would discuss the merits of the article, how it might apply to our jobs, and the issues we were working through.

Sounds so prehistoric, right!? But that's how we brainstormed, shaped our opinions, and shared how it related to us. It got us thinking and expressing ourselves. It helped us grow as individuals and as a team.

And, it was fantastic! We had some great conversations.

Now it's so much easier. We can share something interesting we read and invite conversations with a much larger audience on LinkedIn. I have clients who do what Kevin did but on LinkedIn. They discover an article, share it on LinkedIn, and tag their team. While they are not required to comment on LinkedIn, they dedicate time at least once a month in staff meetings to review the merits of the article.

It's about more than *sharing* or *posting.* It's joining conversations about what other people have posted. This enables you to add your point of view and insights. Perhaps you share some related experiences from earlier in your career or more recently.

This keeps social media social and prevents your corner of LinkedIn from becoming a one-way broadcasting and often-ignored media platform. More importantly, it gives you a chance to develop your voice and demonstrate your leadership and domain expertise, which is *showing*. This helps people relate to you, which enables people to see you as a real human being versus just a name on the top of a resume.

Lastly, commenting on posts helps people connect to you.

All of this is far better than having a bullet point on your resume that says something along the lines of "[Knox] took this six-week leadership certification course from SMU in 2001 as part of his leadership development program at Sabre, Inc."

And remember, what you share and how you frame it can speak volumes about your judgment and strategic thinking.

By engaging regularly on LinkedIn, you establish the habit of *showing*, not just telling. This helps you develop a narrative about your career—your leadership skills, problem-solving skills, insights, and unique perspectives—all things that a static resume can never do.

And, when you do this with consistency over time, your network will see you, your value, your career, your insights, and your leadership skills on a regular basis versus seeing only a static snapshot (your resume) when you send it out to a very limited audience.

Key Point 4: Shifting Your Perspective About LinkedIn

When LinkedIn first arrived on the scene, it was viewed as a job board. Social media was new. Applying to jobs online was new.

When you worked in an office cubicle, it would be terrible optics if you were caught spending time on a job board. Job searches and networking while on the job were also taboo, unless you were in sales.

I remember vividly because the company I worked for at the time started the tradition of layoffs every year in December. As an unintended consequence, every September people started ramping up their networking and job-seeking activities. Everyone became secretive, finding places where they could login to their accounts and hit apply or have private conversations.

Over the years, though, different job boards came and went. Monster.com, Headhunter.net, and CareerBuilder.com are some of the ones that come to mind. But LinkedIn evolved into a true social platform. When LinkedIn is used properly, it is less of a broadcast platform or job board and more of an engagement, learning, and networking platform. It is a platform where conversations can take place, either publicly through posts and comments or privately through direct messages (DMs).

LinkedIn evolved into a place where there are 15 times more informational posts than job posts. This means that people are having conversations about topics related to your areas of expertise, industry, and professional interests.

Framed properly, LinkedIn offers you opportunities to join conversations, and when you do that strategically and intentionally, you network effectively. You can establish your professional presence. You can position yourself as a subject matter expert (SME) and/or thought leader. You can build and nurture relationships.

You can do this so much more effectively than at an in-person networking event where you are limited to initiating a conversation with one person or a small group of people directly in front of you.

This leads us to the perspectives you need to have with LinkedIn and building your digital footprint. We already know (or should know) that the best time to build your presence is not when you are job-hunting. It is *before* you need it.

Why do I say this? Why do I absolutely believe in this principle? Because I have been laid off. I was caught in that yearly Christmas season surprise of my employer who made headcount reductions.

Statistic

- LinkedIn has 15 times more content than job postings. LinkedIn is no longer just a job board. It's a networking and learning machine!

Case Study: Knox Layoff

Out of grad school, I was hired into a leadership development program for a Fortune 500 company, starting as an analyst in their technology division. I was someone with zero technology background. (My undergraduate degree is in English literature with a minor in Spanish and general business; my graduate degree is in Management Information Systems and Finance.)

As part of the leadership development program, I was exposed to senior executives across the organization. Because I worked on the company's foundational technology—technology that drove more than $1bn in annual revenue—I became one of the few people who truly understood how it worked and how it impacted the business.

More importantly, I learned to communicate how that technology worked—and why it mattered—across different functional lenses. The same system meant different things to different groups: Finance cared about cost, risk, and forecasting; operations focused on reliability and scale; sales on speed, differentiation, and customer impact; development on architecture and limitations; executives on strategy and growth; and, eventually, Wall Street on narrative and valuation.

After year one, I received my first promotion. After year two, I received my second promotion. After year three, I received my third promotion and was invited to the CEO's up-and-coming leaders.

I felt that I was on my way. I felt that I was untouchable.

At the end of year four, I transferred departments. At the end of year five? I was laid off.

I was shocked. Upset. I couldn't believe it.

And do you know how long I was unemployed?

Three hours. Yes, only three hours.

How? Why? Because as much as I felt that I was invincible—that there was no way that a company that had a leadership development program (of which I was a part) and someone who was on the fast track to more promotions and more upward mobility and someone was recently part of the CEO's special group—I was wary. Wary of the annual reduction in workforce. Wary of being the new person in a new department (think accounting: last in, first out). So I had kept on networking the old-fashioned way: in person, at breakfasts and lunches, in certification programs, and at alumni and industry association events.

I made sure my resume was up to date, sharing it when people asked and interviewing even though I thought I was secure in my job.

In other words, I continued to build my professional presence (not my personal brand) even when I was not seriously job hunting. I had been laying the foundation for my career safety net. I had leveraged all the tools at my disposal to fuel my opportunity engine.

That's how you should consider everything you do on LinkedIn: as your career safety net and a way to generate new opportunities for your career. While you might spend time on other social media platforms, you need to invest time on LinkedIn. LinkedIn's payoff is far greater than the others.

Key Point 5: You Control Your Narrative

Some people on social media overshare. I'm not telling you to do that. Since your reputation precedes you, this is your chance to shape that reputation. You can create your professional narrative by being strategic and intentional with what you post, who you engage with, what topics you engage with, and how you engage. We will cover this more in Chapter 10 (Build Your Content Framework) and Chapter 9 (Develop Your Persona). Right now I am simply planting the seeds for your interest in doing this.

LinkedIn gives you a platform to tell your story your way. There are no gatekeepers and no need to wait for someone else to pick you. As your own publicist, you are creating the foundations and the stories that define your professional brand.

The topics that you choose to share and engage with automatically tie you to those topics. This is especially important for mid-career professionals, career changers, consultants, or anyone establishing their professional brand. This is equally important for small business owners, too. By consistently adding value to your audiences through your comments and posts, you will naturally differentiate yourself.

Case Study: How Anabella Rewrote the Narrative of Her Business

When Anabella Mainetti launched Mainefactured, her steel-framed tiny home company, she was coming off more than a decade of running a successful marketing agency.

Ironically, despite her marketing background, she admits she dreaded LinkedIn.

"For years, I dismissed LinkedIn as a noisy place full of solicitors," she told me, *"and to be honest, back then I was one of them—sending pushy messages that went nowhere."*

When she started Mainefactured, Anabella knew she couldn't afford to repeat old patterns. Instead of showing up as just another company trying to sell, she showed up as a human being with expertise, curiosity, and a willingness to give without asking.

She built her LinkedIn presence around three simple content pillars:

- Education: explaining why her construction methods were different and why that mattered.
- Authenticity: sharing the real story behind the company—the risks, challenges, and dreams.
- Connection: engaging with other entrepreneurs in a genuine, non-transactional way.

"Once I stopped thinking about selling and started thinking about connecting, everything changed. People began to trust me before they ever spoke to me," Anabella said.

By consistently showing up online in a way that reflected her values and voice, Anabella reshaped how people perceived both her and her business. Leads started coming in from people who already knew her story. That sense of familiarity and trust became Mainefactured's competitive edge.

Why It Matters

Your digital narrative is shaped not just by what you post, but by *how* you show up. Every comment, post, and interaction signals what you stand for, long before someone ever meets you.

Anabella didn't win attention because she shouted louder; she earned trust because she showed up consistently, with clarity, authenticity, and intention.

When people feel like they already know you, they are more likely to trust you, refer you, and buy from you. That's the power of controlling your own narrative online: It turns your presence into a trust accelerator.

Key Point 6: Your Network Has a Network

Another reason to stay active on LinkedIn is simple: *No one can hire or refer you if they can't see you.*

Think of your LinkedIn presence like a storefront. If it looks abandoned, people walk right past. But the moment you start engaging, even through something as small as liking others' posts, then your name starts showing up in other people's feeds.

That tiny ripple matters. When your network scrolls and sees *"[Your Name] liked this post,"* it's a subtle reminder that you're here, active, and part of the conversation.

Over time, those small moments stack up. You move from invisible to familiar, and familiarity builds trust.

Bottom line: Activity creates visibility. Visibility creates opportunity.

Think of being active on LinkedIn as the six degrees of separation game, or six degrees of Kevin Bacon if you know that game. Even LinkedIn shows you the number of degrees of separation that you have from someone.

Less than a generation ago, your Rolodex held the names in your network. Back then, your network was limited to the people you already knew, and maybe they introduced you to other people. It was a more laborious and time intensive process. Today, LinkedIn extends your reach exponentially and much more expediently.

Through second- and third-degree connections, you can access people who would have once been completely unreachable. You can land introductions and opportunities from someone who knows someone who saw a comment you left on a post you didn't even write.

Here's how it works: When you comment thoughtfully on someone's post, your comment is not limited to just the person who posted it or to your own network. It surfaces in their network, too.

You instantly gain visibility with people you likely wouldn't have connected with otherwise. And those people, if intrigued, can click on your name, view your profile, and begin to engage with you directly.

That's the power of visibility. That's the power of being active on LinkedIn.

What makes this so intriguing is that it feels organic. You don't have to cold message a stranger. You don't have to awkwardly ask for introductions. You don't have to get up early for a networking breakfast. Instead, you only have to show up regularly on LinkedIn and add value consistently over time. Let your perspective, support, and expertise create a ripple effect that naturally leads others back to you.

In this sense, LinkedIn acts as an open marketplace of ideas and engagement, not just contact names and a job board. LinkedIn is where your network's network is just a comment away, but only if you're present.

Don't just build a network. Activate it. Check on it. Nurture it. Engage with it.

Engage intentionally with the people you know, and the ones they know will start seeing you, too. The second- and third-degree connections' visibility is one of the platform's most underrated benefits. Like compound interest, it only works if you keep *investing* your time.

This isn't just about getting seen. It's about becoming discoverable and showing up in the right places, with the right energy and for the right reasons. It's about building your professional online reputation.

In short: Your network has a network. If you learn how to engage with that reality in mind, you're no longer playing a solo game. You are expanding your reach without chasing it, and that's when the magic starts to happen.

Knox Tip: Start by leaving one thoughtful comment a day. Just one. Watch how your visibility expands in a matter of weeks.

Key Point 7: You Don't Need to Be a "Content Creator"—Just a Consistent Professional

Let me reemphasize something: You do not need to go viral to win on LinkedIn. Just as importantly, you do not have to create original content other than commenting. Not everyone is meant to be a "content creator," and frankly, most people don't have the time or desire to create original content like blogs.

What truly matters is showing up consistently. That means starting by liking posts and then building into commenting thoughtfully, curating smart articles, and sharing insights from your own work. Each touchpoint signals to your network that you're engaged, informed, and adding value. Over time, those small actions build credibility.

Think of it this way: You're not performing; you are focused on participating. LinkedIn isn't a stage where you need to entertain. It's a conversation where your voice, used consistently and authentically, builds trust. And trust is what gets you noticed, remembered, and eventually contacted.

Exercise

- Have you downloaded the LinkedIn app to your mobile device? If not, do so and start logging in daily.
- Comment on one post per day for seven days. Track how your profile views increase. Also check on how many impressions your comment receives.

Statistics

- 95 percent of recruiters are vetting candidates on LinkedIn before making decisions.
- Companies leveraging LinkedIn to build relationships outperform businesses that don't by 78 percent.
- Professionals with fully optimized LinkedIn profiles are 40 more likely to receive opportunities.

Strategic Effects: Visibility Is a Force Multiplier

When you start to create your own visibility, you start to shape the environment where you will be seen. And when you are seen, you give others the chance to observe you—your expertise, consistency, and values—long before you ever step into a room with them. You shape your professional reputation.

That's the quiet power of Digital Validation™

Small, intentional actions on LinkedIn—a like, comment, or thoughtful post—don't just increase reach. They create a persistent field of visibility where opportunities can find you.

Remember, it is rarely about shouting the loudest. Instead, it's about showing up with intention consistently. Over time, those micro-moments of visibility compound into credibility, trust, and visibility.

Create the environment. Let others observe. Let visibility do the heavy lifting.

Be seen.

Key Takeaways

- LinkedIn is more than a resume or Rolodex; it's your career storefront.
- Static presence = missed opportunities. Active presence = visibility and trust.
- You don't need to go viral. You need to be active and consistent.
- Your network's network is where your opportunity lives.
- Be intentional. Add value. Build trust. Be seen.

QR Code

CHAPTER 5
Your LinkedIn Scorecard

Establish a Baseline

As a management consultant, the first thing we do with any new client or project is conduct a *current state assessment.*

What is that?

It's the power of knowing where you stand.

Before proposing a solution, redesigning a process, or optimizing a system, we need to understand what we're working with. You cannot set a strategy without knowing your starting point. It's like trying to run a marathon without checking where the starting and finishing lines are.

That same logic applies directly to your LinkedIn profile and, more broadly, your digital presence.

Most professionals skip this step. They jump straight to updating headlines, tweaking summaries, or creating content before ever asking the following:

- What story am I telling right now?
- Does my profile reflect who I am today or a past version of me?
- If someone Googled me, would what they find reinforce my credibility or raise questions?

Establishing a baseline is about *orientation*: Step 2 of my Strategic Effects framework. It's the act of pausing long enough to observe where you are, understand how you're being perceived, and analyze the gap between where you are and where you want to be.

When you take time to establish that baseline, everything that follows, including your messaging, content, and engagement, becomes more intentional and aligned.

Digital Validation™ begins with self-awareness.

Before you can control the narrative, you have to know what narrative already exists.

Knox POV: In consulting, we never prescribe before we diagnose. The same applies here: Don't jump into polishing your profile until you've measured your presence honestly.

Why It Matters

If you don't know where you stand, you can't see your own blind spots, and that's where opportunities are lost.

Recruiters, clients, and decision-makers are already forming impressions based on what they find about you online. If that digital reflection is outdated, inconsistent, or incomplete, they'll fill in the blanks on their own and not always in your favor.

Establishing a baseline gives you a clear picture of your digital footprint and a framework to measure progress against. It's how you move from guessing to knowing, from reactive to intentional.

In the Strategic Effects model, this is where you orient and begin to analyze, gathering context before taking action. Once you see your current state clearly, you can chart a course that builds credibility, earns trust, and increases visibility.

Digital Validation™ starts here, with awareness, clarity, and the courage to take an honest look at your professional reflection.

Strategic Effects—The Power of Orientation

In my Strategic Effects framework, this chapter represents the second step: orientation.

After you've observed what's happening around you—the landscape, your peers, and the market—the next move is to orient yourself within it.

That means asking the following:

- Where do I stand right now?
- What do others see when they look for me?
- How does my digital presence compare to the story I want to tell?

Orientation is about context and clarity. You can't improve what you haven't examined.

When consultants step into a new client environment, we start with a current state assessment (CSA), not because it's glamorous but because it's essential.

CSAs give us truth. They tell us what's real, not what we assume.

The same principle applies to your professional presence.

Before optimizing your profile, posting content, or building an audience, you need to know exactly where you stand.

That clarity becomes your compass.

In this chapter, you will orient yourself in the digital landscape, so every action you take from here on out is deliberate, strategic, and aligned with where you want to go.

Orientation is the step where you make sense of what you've observed. It's where you interpret the signals, understand the context, and define the strategy *before* you take action. Because taking action for the sake of action is just motion. Taking intentional, strategic action creates momentum—momentum in the right direction.

Key Message

I've said this before and I will say it again.

Your LinkedIn presence is more than your resume.

LinkedIn is your narrative and storefront. It can be your opportunity to enter rooms and meet people online before you actually even converse with them.

Your LinkedIn profile is how people assess your credibility and expertise and whether they want to work with you.

Yet, most professionals (less than 30 percent) never fully complete their profile. This means that the majority of people have not objectively evaluated their presence either. They either ignore it completely or assume it's okay because they haven't gotten complaints or are not actively looking for a job.

That's not a strategy; that's ignoring the elephant in the room.

If you don't know how you're showing up online, then you can't improve it. You're invisible, or worse—forgettable.

I am about to share with you my proprietary LinkedIn Scorecard. It was built "in the field," not in a conference room. It was designed after working with thousands of profiles in order to effectively communicate someone's gaps with their LinkedIn presence. More importantly, it creates actionable and tangible steps that can help improve it.

This is the foundation for improving your online professional presence.

The LinkedIn Scorecard evolved from real-world experience reviewing more than 8,000 LinkedIn profiles across every kind of professional:

- Executives trying to build thought leadership
- Sales teams needing credibility with prospects
- MBA students competing for top internships
- Entrepreneurs struggling to build legitimacy
- Small businesses needing to prove themselves and gain visibility in their markets
- Mid-level managers trying to position themselves for a promotion or their next opportunity
- People who fear a layoff or were already laid off

Over time, I started seeing patterns. Gaps. Blind spots.

I built a tool that would enable me (and, eventually, others) to quantify their digital presence on LinkedIn, so they know exactly what is working, what is missing, and what to fix.

This scorecard became a core part of my workshops, a foundational piece in my employee advocacy programs, and eventually the foundation for this book and its online course.

It's not just diagnostic. It's directional.

It doesn't just tell you where you are; it shows you how to get better.

(Mini) Case Study

Early in my consulting career, I walked into a client meeting where they wanted to overhaul their customer experience program. When we asked how they currently measured satisfaction, they said, "We don't."

That was the moment I realized that you can't improve what you don't measure. The same applies to your digital presence.

The Scorecard Visual

CATEGORY	TOP SCORE	YOUR SCORE	COMMENTS
HEADSHOT	1	1	Friendly, Professional and Engaging
BANNER IMAGE	1	1	Interesting, Conversation Starter, Utilized Across Social Platforms
HEADLINE	1	1	Goes beyond job title; Descriptive; Show Personality; Up to 220 characters
CONNECTIONS	1	1	500 is baseline
ACTIVITY	2	2	Are you recently *active* on platform? Are you liking, commenting & sharing?
ABOUT (SUMMARY)	2	2	Written in first person; Tells a story; Leverage bullet points & white spaces; Is not generic; Contains Contact Information
JOB DESCRIPTIONS	1	1	While LinkedIn is not a replacement for your resume, you should have 2 - 4 bullets points for each position
CONTACT INFO & OTHER	1	1	Provides an email or phone number. Has Interests, Charities, and Featured Projects
TOTAL	10	10	Excellent

So let's get to it. This is what the scorecard looks like. We'll review each section in a minute, but let's take a high-level look at it. To see and download the full version of the scorecard, please go to the QR section.

The main sections of a profile are: Profile Image, Banner Image, Headline, About (or summary section), Experience, Featured Content, and Skills.

The other, not so obvious ones are number of connections, your contact information, and how active you are on the platform.

All in all, I focus on eight sections: six with a maximum score of 1 and two with a maximum score of 2. Scoring is in increments of 0.5.

The maximum score is 10, and the lowest score is 0. No one hits either of those. Most people score between 3.5–5.5.

The purpose is to show you your baseline and how you can increase your professional online presence and visibility.

I have included a PDF version of the LinkedIn Scorecard in the QR Code section of this chapter. Feel free to download and print it now as you start your analysis.

In this chapter we will be scoring ourselves. In Chapter 6, we will work on improving or optimizing our presence.

Recruiter or Sales Perspective

Before we dive into each section of your LinkedIn profile, consider this: When a recruiter, employer, or potential client (yes, small business owners, potential customers often want to know who they are buying from and what their story is) lands on your profile, they are evaluating you within seconds:

- Is your profile photo professional, warm, and inviting?
- Does your headline communicate value?
- Are you actively adding value and engaging with your network?
- Is your About (summary) section compelling?
- Is your work experience and profile complete?

A half-completed LinkedIn profile sends the wrong message. If you aren't optimizing your presence, you are giving opportunities to someone else.

Statistics

- Recruiters see thousands of resumes each week. They spend an average of six seconds scanning your resume (or LinkedIn profile) to determine whether they are interested in you.
- 95 percent of recruiters leverage LinkedIn to find candidates.
- It's easy to stand out on LinkedIn given that less than 30 percent of the profiles I've seen are fully completed or optimized.

Knox POV: If you do not have a fully optimized LinkedIn profile, you run the risk of being passed over or ignored altogether.

When I grade myself on projects, I am a harsh grader. As you evaluate your LinkedIn profile, you should be a harsh grader, too.

Outside Perspective

Brené Brown once said: "Owning our story and loving ourselves through that process is the bravest thing we'll ever do."

That's what this exercise is really about: owning your professional story before someone else writes it for you.

LinkedIn Scorecard: Section 1—Headshot

Sounds simple, right? But it's not.

Your headshot should be friendly, professional, and engaging. Do you look like a warm person? Or do you look threatening and intimidating?

Does your headshot look like you? Is it recent? If we had never met in person and had only connected on LinkedIn, and we set up an in-person networking meeting at Starbucks, would I recognize you when you walk in?

You would be surprised at how many people look nothing like their profile pictures!

If your headshot is recent and well-lit, with nothing distracting in the background, and it is not AI generated or animated (cartoon like), then give yourself a 1.

If your headshot has someone cropped out of it, multiple people in it, if you are wearing a hat or sunglasses, or if your privacy settings have it blocked, give yourself a 0.

Remember, the first thing that people see is your headshot, and people want to connect with other people. The good news is that we no longer need to have a professional photo done as our smart phones can take excellent pictures!

In Chapters 6 and 7, we will optimize our LinkedIn presence. And, the QR Code section of these chapters provides examples of both what to do as well as what not to do.

Knox Tip: Update your LinkedIn profile photo at least once a year.

LinkedIn Scorecard: Section 2—Banner Image

LinkedIn provides you with a standard, dull gray banner image.

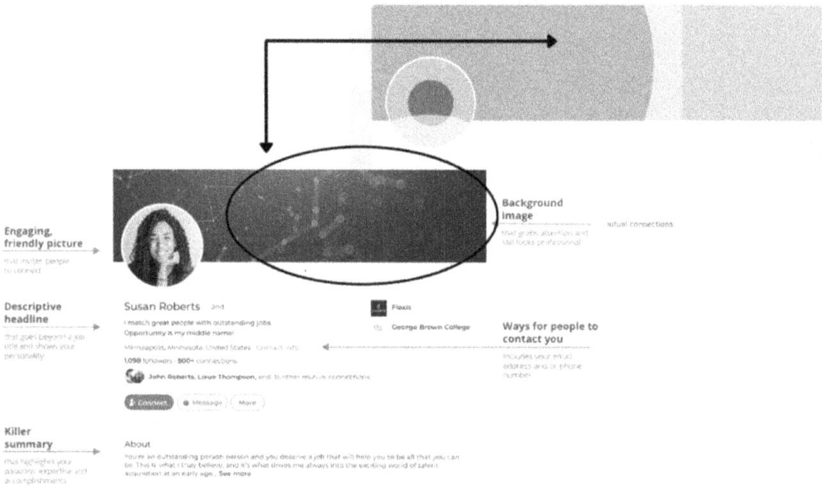

Make it more interesting!

If you're not familiar with what the banner image is, it is the background photo on your LinkedIn profile. Whatever you do, do not use the default.

Your banner image is your first opportunity to share more about yourself. It can be whatever you want it to be. It should be interesting and can be leveraged as a conversation starter.

Now score yourself. If you have a non-default banner image, give yourself a 1. If not, give yourself a 0.

LinkedIn Scorecard: Section 3—Headline

Most people put their job title here. That is a mistake! That information already resides in your Experience section.

Your headline provides you with an opportunity that most people do not take advantage of. LinkedIn provides you with 220 characters for your headline. It is your opportunity to provide insights into who you are and how you think, and to start a conversation.

You can have a job title, but you need to have more than that.

Now score yourself. If you have a job title only in your headline, give yourself a 0.5. No headline: a 0. If your headline utilizes the majority of characters (spaces) and provides interesting information, give yourself a 1.

LinkedIn Scorecard: Section 4—Connections

Under everyone's name on their profile, LinkedIn shows the number of connections up to a maximum of 500.

I believe that if you are on LinkedIn, you are here to connect with people: classmates, colleagues, former colleagues, teachers, friends, clients, and more.

LinkedIn, after all, is *the* professional networking platform. Therefore, at a minimum, you should have at least 500 connections. If not, then you are not taking the platform seriously. You have not demonstrated that you are committed to marketing yourself or your small business.

Now score yourself. If you have 500+ connections, give yourself a 1. If you have less than 500, give yourself a 0. No 0.5s here.

LinkedIn Scorecard: Section 5—Activity

As you scroll down someone's profile, you can see whether they are active on the platform and in what ways they are active. Here's an example of my friend Anabella from Mainefactured, who you were introduced to in a previous chapter.

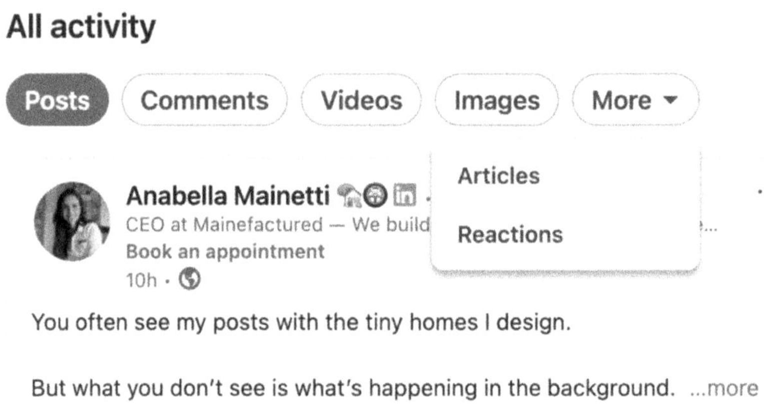

From this you can see *how* she's been active through posts, comments, and reactions (think likes). Being consistently active on LinkedIn increases your visibility on the platform. It draws attention to your posts and your network's posts.

Your activities show up in your contacts newsfeeds. Scrolling through my LinkedIn newsfeed, for example, I can see that Anabella Mainetti liked or commented on a post, and this is true for people with whom I do not have a first-degree connection as well.

In order to stop being a LinkedIn ghost, you need to be active. This means liking, commenting, and sharing.

LinkedIn will also tell you how long ago someone was active on the platform. You can see if their last interaction was three weeks, six months, two years, or even two hours ago.

This is important for two reasons. One, as you network and make new connections, you can immediately get a sense for whether they might respond to a connection request, a post comment, or a DM. If I'm researching someone, for example, and I see that they haven't been active on LinkedIn in the last six months, I will try to find another way to reach out to them.

The same goes for a recruiter or headhunter. If someone finds you interesting and reaches out to you, and you are not regularly logging in to LinkedIn, they may skip you altogether, believing that their efforts will be ignored.

Now score yourself. Keep in mind, 90 percent of people get a 0 here. If you have not been engaged on LinkedIn by even liking other people's posts in the last month, give yourself a 0. If you have been on the platform in the last month and have commented, posted, and liked at least five times, give yourself a 1. If you like posts frequently, comment on posts regularly and share posts at least weekly, give yourself a 2. (Feel free to score a 0.5 or 1.5 as you feel necessary.) Keep in mind, only a handful of people earn a 2.

Statistics

- Currently on LinkedIn, commenting accounts for roughly 80 percent of your visibility from engagement activities.
- Less than 16 percent of LinkedIn members log in on a daily basis.

LinkedIn Scorecard: Section 6—About (Summary)

Your About section is where you get to tell your story: who you are, what you do, and why it matters. This is your opportunity to tell more about who you are as a person. It's your opportunity to differentiate your LinkedIn presence (a narrative) from your resume (a static set of data points).

Here are a few things to keep in mind. You should avoid generic cliched phrases like "hard working" and "passionate." Those words are banal. They do not differentiate you. Our emphasis will always be on show, don't tell.

Also, people do not read any more. Instead, we skim. So, leverage bullet points and white space. Paragraphs should not be more than two sentences.

Again, this is a heavily weighted section in terms of scoring.

Furthermore, you should write your story in first person—leveraging "I." For example: "I've applied this across 30+ years of product management, process reengineering, organizational change management, learning & development, and marketing."

Avoid writing your About section in third person. For example: "Knox Keith has applied this knowledge across 30+ years of work."

The third-person style feels formal, distant, and outdated, and it creates unnecessary separation between you and the reader.

Lastly, you should include at least one way to connect, such as your email address or phone number, in your About section. Even if you have it in your Contact Information, include it here, too. You want it to be easy for hiring managers and recruiters to reach you.

Now score yourself. No About section or the bare minimum, give yourself a 0. If you have more than the bare minimum, and it's not filled with meaningless cliches, give yourself a 1. If your About section is interesting, contains bullet points, is personal, shows personality, leverages keywords, and has at least one way to contact you, then give yourself a 2.

Again, much like the Activity section, most people score a 0 or 1 here. And feel free to score a 0.5 or 1.5 as you feel necessary. Also, only a handful of people score a 2 here.

LinkedIn Scorecard: Section 7—Experience

While I maintain that LinkedIn is not your online resume, you must have one to three bullets for each job listed. Most people provide a date range, a company name, and perhaps a job title in their Experience section and nothing more.

Think of your LinkedIn job descriptions as an appetizer. Your resume is the full meal, so you do not need to include everything that would be on your resume in your Experience section.

Your Experience section cannot tell your whole professional journey. It should show some of your experience. Highlight some interesting projects. Show results.

Your Experience section should lead someone to want to have a conversation with you and ask you for your full resume.

On LinkedIn, this section should provide enough information to give people an idea of your duties, responsibilities, and achievements.

For small business owners and entrepreneurs, you can position it as part of your story as well as the markets and industries you service.

Simply doing the bare minimum is not enough. And, when I see the bare minimum on someone's profile, I immediately dis-validate (or disqualify them).

Now score yourself. If you have the bare minimum and no description of your duties, responsibilities, or accomplishments, give yourself a 0. If you provide one to three bullet points per job listed and you describe your responsibilities, give yourself a 1. Anything in between, give yourself a 0.5.

LinkedIn Scorecard: Section 8—Other

For my Other section, I look for three things:

- Contact information
- Featured projects
- Charities / volunteer work

You will hear me say this multiple times: I am amazed by the number of people who will try to leverage the "Open to Work" label on their profile photo, yet provide no contact information. You want to be immediately dis-validated? Try sending out your resume with no contact information! This is the same thing on LinkedIn.

How do you expect a recruiter or hiring manager who is looking at multiple people to contact you if you provide no contact information? If you are not active on LinkedIn, then your direct messages are useless. If your contact information doesn't exist, then I'm moving on to the next person.

Admittedly, everyone may not be able to see your contact information based on LinkedIn, how many degrees of separation, and your privacy settings. So make sure you provide an email address and/or phone number in your About section just in case!

Your LinkedIn profile also has a Featured Project Section. Show some of your work! Provide a conversation starter! One of my featured projects is a video that I helped produce and was tagged on it by the videographer. Those projects are definite conversation starters.

As for charities, don't *say* that you have a "passion for animal welfare." Instead, *show* that it is important to you by connecting to the Society for the Prevention of Cruelty to Animals (SPCA) and providing the years that you volunteered there as well as a description of what you did.

People are looking for ways to connect with you, whether that is through an alma matter, a charity, or a hobby. When you provide that information, you are giving others a chance to find common ground with you.

Add Up Your Scores

Now add up your score. How did you do? Were you a hard grader?

Most people score between 3.5–5.5. Everyone has room for improvement.

Don't worry too much about your score right now. We will work on optimizing your LinkedIn presence and building your strong, consistent, and professional presence throughout the rest of this book.

Why This Matters

Here are some things to think about:

- If someone lands on your LinkedIn, are you providing them with clarity or confusion?
- Does your headline help them understand you, your values, and your mindset in three seconds or less?
- Is your About section telling a story or putting them to sleep?

People judge. And they judge fast. Recruiters, clients, and potential collaborators don't always give you a second look.

Your profile needs to be more than "complete." It needs to be compelling and current, and you need to show up consistently on a daily basis. You may not currently be looking for a new opportunity, but when you are looking, it's often too late. The networking activities and your active profile needs to be working for you. After all, I would have never been contacted about a pet-project for Michael Dell if I had not been visible on LinkedIn.

You need to make a habit of logging into LinkedIn multiple times a week. You should not come across as someone just going through the motions.

If you are part of the 84 percent of people who do not log in daily, then you are irrelevant and invisible on LinkedIn. Chances are you:

- Are static with your presence.
- Provide zero conversation starters.
- Do not create a living narrative.
- Are inactive on the platform.
- Do not engage in conversations.
- Use cliched and trite language.
- Do the bare minimum.

LinkedIn is a powerful tool, but only when you show up regularly and take advantage of the opportunities it offers.

That's what this scorecard is designed for: to help you assess where you can make improvements, providing you with a map of where to go and what to do next. It's not meant to shame you. It's designed to give you a baseline. A truth-telling mirror. A place to start.

Because once you see the gaps, you can build a plan to close them and start turning up your visibility.

QR Code

CHAPTER 6
Optimize Your LinkedIn—Part 1

This is a long chapter. So long that I decided to break it into Part I and Part II. I also advise that after reading each scoring section of the LinkedIn Scorecard you go to the QR Code section in order to see the additional visuals.

The goal is to show you how each component of your LinkedIn profile can be fully optimized.

Time to Get to Work

Alright, look at your scorecard grade from Chapter 5. How did you do? What was your score? Are you satisfied with where you are, or do you see some opportunities to improve?

I hope it's the latter! That's why you're here after all.

Knox POV:

"If people won't recognize you at Starbucks, it's time to update your profile picture."

Breaking Down the Scoring

I've said it before, and I'll say it again. LinkedIn is not your resume. It's your digital storefront, open 24/7, ready to welcome (or repel) the very people who could change your business, career, or your life.

In the last chapter, I introduced my proprietary LinkedIn Scorecard, designed for you to establish a solid baseline on where you stand with your LinkedIn presence.

Let's breakdown the scoring:

0 - 3.0	You have been cutting your knees out from underneath you. But don't despair. We will get your score up in no time!
3.5 - 5.5	This is where most people land. You are average, and that's okay. With a few key improvements your visibility will expand.
5.5 - 7.5	You are off to a fantastic start! Generally speaking, there are still a few things you can do for some quick wins.
8.0 - 9.0	No one scores above a 9.0, at least not very often. You're doing great! Congrats! Let's hone in and see how you can take advantage of all the good things going for you.

For the rest of this chapter (parts 1 and 2), we will conduct a deep dive into each section, looking for the good and the bad. (Sometimes you can learn more from what not to do!) As a supplement to this chapter, the QR Code provides vibrant examples of both the good and bad.

I will also share stories, examples, and a few hard truths. Whether you're an entrepreneur trying to grow your visibility, a small business owner hoping to attract more customers, or just someone tired of being invisible online, this chapter is your blueprint.

We're going to review the Digital Validation™ Scorecard together. Section by section. With stories. With do's, don'ts, and "oh no they didn't" examples.

Most people score between 3.5–5.5. Everyone has room for improvement.

Don't worry too much about your score right now. We will work on optimizing your LinkedIn presence and building your strong, consistent, and professional presence throughout the rest of this book.

Outside Perspective

Erik Qualman famously said in his book *Socialnomics*:

> *"We don't have a choice on whether we do social media. The question is how well we do it."*
>
> Erik Qualman

This quote from 2009 still holds true today, especially if you replace *social media* with *LinkedIn*. Your LinkedIn profile is your first impression to most of the professional world. Whether you're actively looking for a job or not, people are Googling you, and your profile is doing the talking.

Key Takeaway

Optimize intentionally because silence still speaks volumes.

Strategic Effects

If Chapter 5 was about orienting, understanding where you are, then Chapter 6 is where we move into the next two steps of the Strategic Effects Framework: analyze and act.

Here's why: Think of each section of your LinkedIn profile as a signal, proof point, and piece of your professional narrative.

In this chapter, we're not just looking at those sections; we're taking a hard, honest view at how well they're working for you and then making the changes needed to optimize your presence.

But here's the key: These changes are not permanent. Digital Validation™ is a living, breathing process. Just like your career evolves, so should your LinkedIn. This is where the repeat step comes in.

You should revisit your profile periodically: when your role shifts, when your priorities change, or even just to test new approaches. Personally, I often run two- to four-month campaigns with my LinkedIn profile that focus on my current projects. Examples include creating awareness around Digital Validation™ Course, market research, availability windows for fractional work, and more.

Remember, your LinkedIn profile isn't carved in stone. It's more like clay: shapeable, adaptable, and capable of reflecting where you are right now and where you're going next.

Section 1—Profile Picture (Headshot)

Why It Matters

We now connect with more people online versus the real world or in real life (IRL). A study by HeadShots, Inc. revealed that swapping a low-quality photo for a professional headshot increased perceived competence by 76 percent, likability by 9 percent, and influence by 62 percent. That's a dramatic shift in just one visual cue.

Additional data underscores the power of visuals: LinkedIn profiles with a photo receive up to 21 times more profile views and nine times more interactions compared to those without a proper image.

I want you to take your headshot seriously. It is part of your first impression, just like a good, strong handshake. Before people read a word about you, they are looking at your face. Remember, people connect with people, so what does your profile photo say about you? Is your picture engaging and friendly? Are you clearly visible in the photo?

The headshot sounds simple, and it should be. But most people do not know how to take a good picture.

Sometimes it's easier to learn from seeing what not to do. I know I certainly learned how to be a good manager by having so many bad managers in my career, but those stories are for a different day.

Let's look at some examples of what not to do. Skim down to the QR Code for this chapter, and scan it. I have provided plenty of examples of what to avoid. Here is a partial list from those photos of what not to do:

- Distracting background, such as neon lights or cluttered office.
- A photo where you have clearly cut someone out of the photo.
- Having family members such as a spouse or child in the photo.
- AI photos, cartoons, and caricatures.
- "Sexy" or seductive photos.
- Dated photos (example, photos more than three years old).
- Sports or team / fan related.
- Hats and sunglasses.
- Selfies.
- Events.
- Distorted photos.
- Poor angles.

- Hands covering face.
- Earbuds or headphones.
- Alcohol.
- Looking angry or upset.
- Masks and helmets.
- Photos with celebrities.
- Use of filters.

I know that's a lot of don't's! But I've seen even more!

Case Study: Unrecognizable Executive

I once worked with an executive who I had never met in real life. While I was at a conference, a woman I didn't recognize came up to me and started talking to me as if she had known me for years. It took me a good 10 minutes before I realized who it was. It was the executive.

I didn't recognize her because her profile picture had been over-filtered, so much so that the real-life version of her did not match to the online version of her. It was off-putting and jarring to say the least.

Side story: This always reminds of a meme video where a sheriff is issuing a public service announcement. In the video he pleas for people to stop using filters and AI photos because if you happen to go missing, then no one will be able to recognize you. Lol.

Knox POV: The same goes for your professional presence. I call it the Starbucks test. If I'm meeting you for the first time at Starbucks after we've been engaging online, and I do not recognize you, then you have a problem with your profile picture.

Best Practices

It's so much easier now to take a professional headshot than it was a few years ago. Back in the day, one of my side hustles was shooting headshots. I used a DSLR camera and edited the photos before sending them out.

Now, with the average smart phone, good lighting, and a great smile, you can come away with a fantastic photo. That is, you no longer need professional editing software like Adobe's Photoshop or Lightroom. Instead, I use an app called Snapseed. (Link is in QR Code section.) It has easy editing features and presets built for you.

The other best practice I have is to update my headshot every year. Why? Well, right now I gain more gray hairs each year, so I want to make sure that people recognize me. And, I can immediately tell when one of my photos is outdated based on those gray hairs in my beard and head.

For women, I recommend that you consider updating your profile picture whenever you change a hair color or hairstyle.

Final words on your headshot: Aim for the following:

- Clean background.
- Good lighting.
- Approachable smile (look up Duchenne smile).
- No props unless they are intentional and on-brand.

Homework / To Do:

Upload a new headshot. Ask yourself these questions: Would someone recognize me if they passed me in a coffee shop? Do I look approachable in this photo?

Section 2—Banner Image

Why It Matters

Most people do not choose their own banner image. So they have the LinkedIn assigned generic grey background—the universal sign of "I didn't bother." This helps them remain invisible, and that's a missed opportunity to tell your story visually.

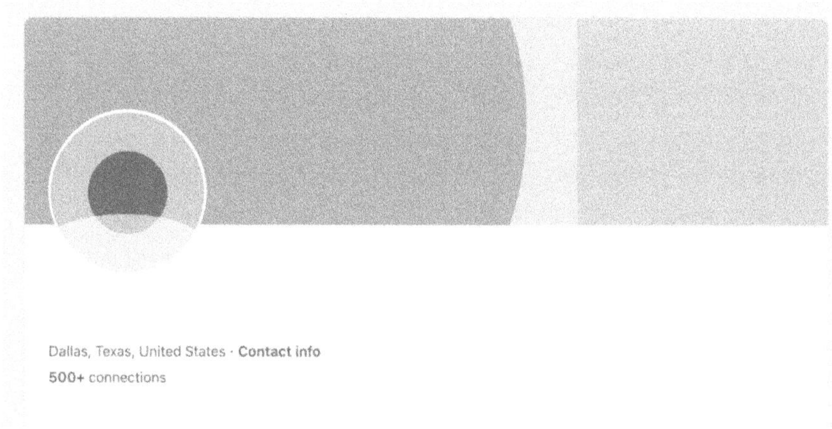

Instead, think of your banner image as your own personal billboard! You can put whatever you want on it to share something about you, what you're doing, or things you support or are interested in. It is an opportunity to differentiate yourself from everyone else. It is another opportunity to create another conversation starter and connect with someone else.

Case Study

One business owner who I worked with used a photo of a country setting with a pond, farmhouse, and some trees. The photo looked very artistic.

Seeing the photo sparked a conversation that we would not have had otherwise. I asked her where the photo was from. It was of her grandparents' farm. We then talked about our grandparents living out in the country and spending summers fishing with our grandfathers, something we later coined "camp grandma and grandpa!" We discovered that we were both amateur photographers, and, as a result, we formed a new and deeper connection.

All from a banner image! Why? Because it sparked a conversation and offered an opportunity to connect on a different level.

Statistics

- Profiles with a customized background banner are 11 times more likely to be viewed than those without one.

That's a powerful validation: Something beyond the default gray significantly boosts visibility.

A background image that resonates can make a profile more engaging and encourage longer visits, increasing the chance visitors explore your experience and skills. One of our goals with a fully optimized LinkedIn presence is to keep visitors on your profile. Previously, I provided a statistic that headhunters on average spend only six seconds scanning someone's resume or CV, so any opportunity to get someone to spend more time on your profile (or LinkedIn storefront) is a win!

Visual elements, especially the banner, significantly shape first impressions.

Here's what you can do:

- Use high-resolution imagery (LinkedIn recommends 1584×396 px).
- Choose visuals that align with your professional brand.
- Consider subtle overlays (company logo, contact info, or tagline) if appropriate, but keep it clean.

- Make sure the area to the left behind your profile photo isn't too busy or distracting.

Here are some ideas for quick impact:

- Personal or hometown landmarks (skyline).
- Industry-related visuals (e.g. tools, workspace).
- Hobbies, creative shots, or favorite sports.
- Memorable vacation scene with meaning.
- Branded banners with your tagline or colors (tastefully executed).
- Favorite sports team.

Quick Win: Change your banner image to something that is interesting, colorful, or industry related. It takes less than three minutes and instantly upgrades your first impression.

Section 3—Headline

Why It Matters

Your headline is the first set of words people see under your profile picture and name. Your headline is your first opportunity to describe who you are.

Far too many people limit their headline to their current job title. When they do, they are doing themselves a huge disservice.

Why? One, because your job title is already listed below in your Experience section. Two, because LinkedIn offers you 220 characters to add more than just your job title. So simply putting manager or senior analyst does nothing to set you apart from your competitors. Instead, you fall into the trap of providing nothing more than the bare minimum.

Let me give you an example. Here is my headline as of September 2025:

Knox Keith
Author - Validated: Add Value. Build Trust. Be Seen (Mar 2026) | Fractional Executive | Speaker & Course Creator | Build Social Proof for Small Businesses & Professionals | Challenge Status Quo | Emmy-Winning Storyteller

Let's walk through this. My headline could say: president or consultant. Those are two of my job titles. Others include lecturer, entrepreneur / small business owner, and board member.

All of those give a vague or generic picture of who I am. It does not convey my work philosophy or what my future looks like. Your headline only having a job title, positions your LinkedIn presence as static, much like your resume. But a fully optimized LinkedIn presence is not static. It is living. Vibrant. It tells a story.

If I relied on job title alone as my headline, I would only be telling people a limited amount of information about me. But by utilizing the full 220 characters, I can offer more conversation starters and insights into how I work. I *show* people who I am. I craft a story and narrative about where I'm going. I build a stronger professional brand and share the vision of where I'm going and who I'm becoming.

Back to my headline. Let's run through each piece of it.

- Author: Have I published this book yet? No. Thus the "coming soon." It shows one of my current projects. It shows aspiration and confidence. (Confidence that it will get done! Lol.).
- Fractional Executive: describes a few of my consulting roles.
- Speaker & Course Creator: is another role of mine.
- Helping Small Businesses & Professionals Build Social Proof: describes one of the anchors of my work—creating *social proof* or *validation* for someone's business or career.

- Challenging the Status Quo: reveals one of the pillars of my Strategic Effects framework
- Emmy-Winning Storyteller: shows one success in my career

Outside Perspectives

"The best way to predict the future is to create it."

—Peter Drucker

"Life isn't about finding yourself.
Life is about creating yourself."

—George Bernard Shaw

Instead of just putting *consultant* in my headline, I instead choose to *show* more details around the roles I've had, the mindsets I follow, and where I am going as part of my career.

This headline is not static. It's not looking toward the past. It is future facing.

- Additionally, one of my goals is to give anyone scanning or reading my LinkedIn profile *anchors* or conversation starters if they want to engage with me. I have provided a ton of opportunities for this by leveraging the full 220 characters that LinkedIn offers in this section and by moving beyond a boring and limiting job title-only headline.

This helps position me as someone who would be interesting to talk to:

- Tell me about your fractional roles
- What gave you the idea to create a course?
- Where do you speak?
- Tell me about your social proof ideas. Why is it important to you?
- How on earth did you win an Emmy?

Knox POV:

"Facts tell. Stories sell."

People long for connection with other people, and stories are the perfect way to connect and make you more memorable. So leverage your headline and, later, your About sections to do that!

Quick Win: Rewrite your headline to show your *value*, not just your title. (I help ___ do ___ beats director of sales.)

Statistics

- Stories are up to 22 times more memorable than facts alone.
- In Chip and Dan Heath's *Made to Stick*, they note that after a presentation, 63 percent of people remember stories, while only 5 percent remember statistics.

Now take a look at your headline. Is it just your job title? Do you utilize the full 220 characters? Does it tell part of your story or is it just a boring snapshot of your past? Is it interesting? Does it spark a conversation?

If not, let's change that!

Exercise / Mini-Workshop: Section 3—Headline

Answer these questions to help draft your new headline.

1. What problems do you solve?

   Example: "I help small businesses grow their audience through strategic social content."

2. Who do you serve?

   Example: "I support healthcare execs navigating organizational change."

3. What results do you deliver?

   Example: "I tripled qualified leads in 90 days through brand strategy + lead magnets."

4. What do people *say* about working with you?

   Example: Use phrases from testimonials or reviews.

5. What differentiates your style or mindset?

   Example: "Challenger of Status Quo | EmpatheticLeader | Data-Informed Storyteller."

For Small Business Owners & Entrepreneurs

Let's be real. You are not just the owner; you are the marketer, the operator, the culture, and the voice of your brand.

So, your headline should reflect that.

Here's a bad example:

"Owner at Tina's Treats"

Now here's a better one:

"Owner @ Tina's Treats 🍪 | Baking joy one cookie at a time | Custom orders | Local pickup | Let's talk sweets!"

The second one is personal. It's specific. It's *you*.

Knox POV: People don't buy from businesses; they buy from humans.

Other Ideas for Headlines

The goal of your headline must be to give someone more information about who you are, your capabilities, how you work, and what you can do. Here are some ideas to help you rewrite and reposition yourself:

1. Give readers your elevator pitch. Example: I help purpose-driven Hoosiers grow their career with Indiana State Government, no matter the career path.
2. Share something personal to make yourself more approachable. Example: Just your friendly neighborhood recruiter | Nerd at heart | Introvert living in an industry of extroverts.
3. Shift the focus to the candidate. Example: *Empowering people to change their lives; driving learning & development as well as growth.*
4. Connect the dots between your employer and corporate brands. Example: *tech recruiter at The Walt Disney Company. Imagine the possibilities ...*
5. Use buzzwords to highlight your skills. Example: *Foundations recruiter at Airbnb | career match-maker | Unicorn hunter.*
6. Ditch the buzzwords for something memorable. Example: *Searching for brave minds to help us reimagine healthcare. Join us and make a difference!*
7. Ask rhetorical questions to encourage the response you want. Example: *17 new public accounting jobs! Want me to review or edit your resume? Need some candidate therapy? DMs are open.*
8. Project confidence and don't be afraid to use emoticons. Example: *Talent acquisition leader, author, and possibly your future colleague!* 😊
9. Focus on the bigger picture. Example: *Build the teams that shape Google's future.*
10. Be bold and take a calculated risk. Example: *I don't usually stalk profiles, but when I do I usually have a career opportunity for you. Want to connect?*

If you want to see other examples of headlines, you can find the link to them in the QR Code section below.

Section 4—Connections

Why It Matters

LinkedIn cuts off its public counting and display of contacts at 500. Therefore, 500+ is the social proof line.

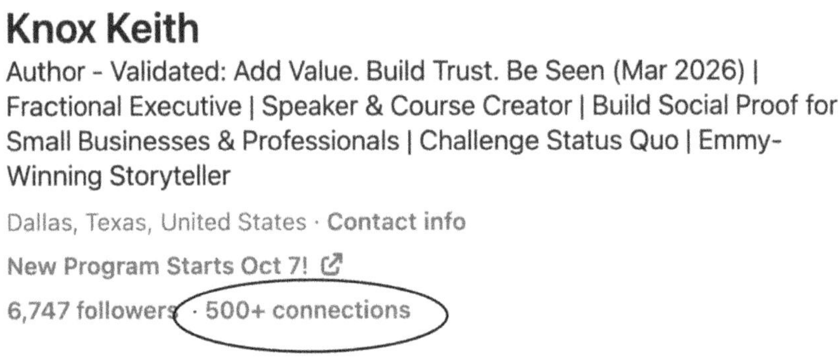

If you have 500+ connections it *shows* me that you have invested in LinkedIn, that you have actively networked to get to 500.

As someone who has had a role as a marketing executive, I judge potential job candidates by this number. If they had reached the 500 number, then I felt like they have adequately marketed themselves professionally. (Yes, exceptions are made, especially for less experienced candidates.) As a consulting executive, new sales are always important, too. I would also judge potential consulting candidates under the same light.

And if we spin this perspective a little, a minimum of 500 LinkedIn connections is also a form of Digital Validation™ in that if you have at least 500 connections, then a significant number of people see value in being connected to you!

Regardless of whether you have 500 connections, you should leverage LinkedIn as an opportunity to connect with people. Here are some easy ways to connect:

1. Connect with your coworkers.
2. At conferences, ditch the business card collection. Instead, open the LinkedIn app, and connect there instead. See the visual steps in the QR Code for this section.
3. Alumni: Alumni connections often share a common bond, background, or experience, making it easier to establish rapport.
4. Recruiters and HR professionals: These professionals should be the ultimate networkers and connectors as they constantly seek job candidates. Naturally, these relationships can lead to potential job opportunities or valuable insights into the hiring process. [Reminder: The best time to network is when you do not need a job, so establishing and nurturing relationships with this category/type can be important to your future successes.]
5. Mutual connections: Looking for and leveraging mutual connections can facilitate introductions and grow your network more organically.
6. Local networking groups: Attending networking events can facilitate connections with like-minded professionals.
7. Industry peers: Connect with colleagues from past or current workplaces, industry events, or professional organizations.
8. Thought leaders: Follow and connect with thought leaders and subject matter experts by engaging with their content and sharing your insights.
9. Targeted outreach: Identify individuals or companies you admire or with whom you would like to collaborate, and send personalized connection requests.
10. Content creators: Engage with individuals who regularly share valuable content related to your industry or expertise. Liking, commenting, and sharing their posts can spark conversations and opportunities to connect.

11. Engage with connection requests: Actively review and respond to incoming connection requests. Personalized messages expressing genuine interest in connecting can help establish rapport and foster meaningful connections.
12. Consistent engagement: Regularly engage with your network by sharing valuable content, participating in discussions, and congratulating connections on professional achievements. Consistent engagement helps keep connections active and strengthens relationships over time.

Statistics

- LinkedIn states that 80 percent of your visibility on the platform is derived from engaging (or commenting) on other people's posts. [Note: You need to say more than "Great job" or "Congratulations." You need to go beyond the auto-generated responses that LinkedIn provides.]

Knox Perspective: Building and maintaining online professional relationships takes time. Be patient. Invest time weekly, if not daily.

Add a note to connection requests. This is simple and should not be complicated.

Example: *Hi Sarah, it was great to meet you at the brand innovators event during SxSW. Enjoyed your insights on how AI is impacting marketing. Look forward to future discussions!—Knox*

Outside Perspective: Ted Rubin

In a blog post back in 2014, Ted wrote: *"If you don't include a personal note when you reach out to connect here on LinkedIn ... the odds are I will ignore and delete the request."*

Ted goes on to say: *"I like to connect if there's potential for mutual value ... If that value isn't obvious a note always helps to add context."*

So here's the core idea: When sending out a connection request on LinkedIn (or any professional network) include a personalized note rather than a generic *"I'd like to connect."* It shows intent, relevance, and respect for the recipient's time.

Case Study: Nicholas moving to Austin

When Nicholas Calvi moved from Milan to Austin to pivot from fashion into tech, he did what most people do at first: He fired off 50+ online applications.

The result? Silence. Not a single meaningful response.

He described the process as "dehumanizing."

And he's not wrong; blind applications usually are.

Everything changed when he stopped applying and focused on *connecting*. Nicholas shifted his strategy:

1. Identified a handful of target companies.
2. Researched the people who worked there.
3. Looked for real points of connection.
4. Engaged in a human way.

And that's when he found her. At one of his top-choice companies, a woman in a senior version of the role he wanted had spent one semester abroad at his university, Bocconi in Milan, a school nearly no one in the US recognizes, as Nicholas joked in our interview: "*In Europe it's an advantage. Here it's almost a disadvantage because people have no idea what it is.*"

But she knew. And that's all that mattered. He reached out with a simple message grounded in shared humanity, not a resume: "*I saw you studied at Bocconi. I went there too. I'd love to learn more about your experience at the company.*"

That tiny overlap—a school, a semester, a place no one else understood—created an instant bridge. She replied. They talked.

Later, when an opportunity arose, she remembered Nicholas and referred him. And later, the company hired him.

Key Takeaway

People connect through stories, shared experiences, and human details, not job titles. Your profile, connection requests, posts, and comments should give someone a reason to say, "*Oh, you're one of my people.*"

Entrepreneur POV

One of my clients owns several locations of a takeout-only restaurant franchise. Since there are no dine-in options, catering is a major growth driver. To break into the sub-markets of his city, Mike knew he had to become the face of the brand.

Once the operations were stable, Mike focused on building real relationships with the people who could open doors: neighborhood schools and parent organizations, churches, city councils, networking groups, event planners, and more.

But here's the key: Mike didn't just send a generic email blast. He showed up. He introduced himself. He sent personal notes. He made the effort to be seen, heard, and remembered. He did this in person and online.

Within six months, Mike wasn't chasing business; business was coming to him. His food became a staple at local gatherings, and he was being referred to new contacts before he even had to ask.

Why this Matters

Building meaningful connections requires effort. It's not about "collecting" people on LinkedIn; it's about cultivating real relationships that drive visibility, trust, and opportunity. Mike didn't just connect; he activated his network.

Key Takeaway

If you want more inbound opportunities—job offers, speaking engagements, referrals, or clients—you can't sit behind a screen and hope people find you. You have to show up, personalize, and follow through.

That's how your connections become your biggest advocates.

Knox POV: One of the keys to networking is to be interested and be interesting. You should ask questions of your contacts and share valuable perspectives. You cannot just focus on what you need at the moment. Networking is a time to get to know the other person and see how you can help them.

I told you this chapter was long! And we're only at the halfway point with your LinkedIn Scorecard. Let's take a break here. Review the visual examples in the QR Code section. Spend some time thinking about how you want to improve your LinkedIn presence.

When you're ready, we can jump into Part II.

QR Code

CHAPTER 7

Optimize Your LinkedIn—Part II

What We Covered in Part I

So far, below are the sections of your LinkedIn Scorecard that we have covered:

- Headshot
- Banner Image
- Headline
- Connections

In Part II, we will cover:

- Activity
- About (Summary)
- Job Descriptions
- Contact Info & Other

As with Part I, you can scan the link in the QR Code section to see visuals for each of the remaining sections.

Now that we've worked on making a strong first impression with your banner and headline, the next step is where trust really builds: your About section.

Section 5—About (Summary)

Why It Matters

This is your chance to sound like a human being and an opportunity to share far more (and thus connect more) than a resume ever can.

Your About section (sometimes I call it summary) is the one place where you can define yourself in your own words, free of start dates and titles. You can leverage it to put career choices in context, highlight your biggest achievements, and show off your personality.

Many people barely do the minimum here. Hell, some people don't even *have* an About section!

Perhaps the reason for this is that so many of us were conditioned to the limitations of the traditional one-to-two-page resume or CV. And for many years, if not decades, we were taught to have a couple of lines at the top of our resumes for goals or objectives.

You need to get out of this mindset! You need to fully leverage your About section in order to fully position yourself as a complete professional, thought leader, subject matter expert, or valuable employee.

Here's a list of why a LinkedIn About section is important:

- Provides a positive and professional first impression.
- Differentiates you in your own words from the crowd.
- Enables you to build emotional connection.
- Helps you drive higher engagement.
- Showcases your skills, capabilities, and achievements.
- Offers you the opportunity to go beyond dates and facts; gives you a chance to share your mindset and perspectives.
- Builds trust.

A good LinkedIn summary effectively communicates your *professional* identity. To do this it needs to be engaging and professional and incorporate elements of your professional branding as part of your Digital Validation™.

A good LinkedIn About section avoids cliches. It shares more about you other than just your job role or title. It helps humanize your online presence.

A good LinkedIn summary is written in the first person. It uses white space, making it easier to skim. (Remember, people do not read anymore. I know, I know, the irony that I'm saying that in a book! Perhaps you're listening to this on Audible as opposed to reading it. Oh, and bullet points are your friend. No paragraph should be longer than two sentences.)

A good LinkedIn About section is rich with keywords relevant to your career space and industry.

It also contains your contact information.

By comparison, what are the components of a poor About section?

- No summary
- The bare minimum
- Cliched or generic phrases
- Written in the third person
- Long paragraphs
- No keywords
- No contact information

Your About section is where you sell yourself by giving insights into who you are, where you've been, and where you're going. And you can do this without sounding like a pushy used-car salesperson!

Your About section provides a great opportunity for you to *show* more (don't tell) about who you are and your mindset. As you build your professional brand, you must take advantage of these opportunities and move beyond the generalities and cliches of the average profile.

In doing so, you will find new ways to connect with your network and position yourself throughout your career.

Tell your story and why you love what you do. Utilize keywords. Add bullet points. Keep it skimmable.

Knox POV: See the QR Code section for my free download: 75 Cliched Phrases to Avoid. Too many people describe themselves with phrases that are common and generic. Words like *hardworking* and *passionate* come to mind. Overused or cliched phrases make you invisible. Stop telling. Start showing.

Mini Case Study: Sonia—The About Section That Did the Heavy Lifting

Sonia, a mid-career professional pivoting from operations to strategy, came to me convinced she needed a "personal branding overhaul." What she really needed was clarity.

We focused on her headline and about sections—not to stuff them with buzzwords, but to tell a clear, professional story. Instead of a list of job titles, we framed her expertise, impact, and focus areas in plain language.

Within two months, recruiters she did not know were visiting her profile and sending her DMs. She hadn't changed her job, skills or network, just the way she told her story.

Key Takeaway

Clarity beats cleverness. A well-crafted About section is your digital elevator pitch.

Statistics

- Profiles with a fully completed About section get up to three times more views.
- Recruiters are two-and-a-half times more likely to contact candidates with a keyword-rich About section.
- LinkedIn users spend an average of 30 seconds longer on profiles with a well-written About section.
- Including contact information in your About section can increase inbound outreach by 35 percent.
- Profiles with bullet points or structured formatting in About sections are 40 percent more likely to convert profile views into connection requests or messages.

Outside Perspective

"The most human company wins."

—Mark Schaefer, Author of *Known*

I think that applies to LinkedIn as well. The most human LinkedIn profile wins, too!

Why It Matters

Your About section isn't just a summary; it is your handshake, opening line, and first impression. People don't build trust with resumes; they build trust with humans. By showing personality, sharing your perspective, and telling a clear story, you are giving people something to connect to emotionally. That's what drives visibility, trust, and ultimately, opportunity. In a world full of noise, being human stands out.

Mini Case Study

One of my students rewrote her About section to highlight why she cares about healthcare innovation. Within two months, she was approached by a recruiter for a role she hadn't even applied for. Her experience didn't change; her story did. And it was her story that resonated with the recruiter.

Strategic Effects

LinkedIn should never be seen as a set-it-and-leave-it platform. As you and your career evolve, so too should your LinkedIn profile. This is especially true for your About section. As your career evolves, revisit and refine it. This is the repeat step in Strategic Effects. Your story should grow with you.

Outside Perspective

"Good writing serves the reader, not the writer. It isn't self-indulgent. It's generous."

—Ann Handley

Your About section isn't about showing off; it's about building a bridge between who you are and what your audience needs to understand about you.

In grad school, we were taught to bridge the gap between the requirements of a role and our own experience. If the job required "A," and we hadn't done exactly "A," we had to articulate *how* our skills and achievements translated to that need.

The same principle applies here. A strong About section meets your reader where they are. It connects your story, skills, and perspective to the problems they need solved. That's what generous writing does: invites people in and helps connect you.

Section 6—Activity

Why It Matters

If you haven't posted or commented in months, you will come across as missing in action or MIA. Being active on LinkedIn drives your visibility. Inactive profiles are like ghost towns. They look abandoned and get little attention.

Your activity is key to becoming discoverable or visible on LinkedIn.

This means logging in daily. It means investing time scrolling through your news feed and at a minimum liking posts in your feed.

Not all activities are weighted equally. You might think that posting content would get you noticed. But one statistic reveals that only 10 percent of our visibility on LinkedIn is generated from posting, while 80 percent is generated from our comments.

Why is this?

My theory is that social media is supposed to be *social.* That means engaging in conversations, i.e., commenting on posts. Posting is just broadcasting; it's one-dimensional until someone engages with the post.

Most of the business world falls into this trap: They only broadcast their messages, which means that their social media is not social. It's just another form of media, which is easy to ignore. The real value is for companies to build employee advocacy programs and create well-orchestrated, value-oriented campaigns designed for true engagement.

But we will save the employee advocacy conversations for my second book! Wink.

How do you know when someone is *active* on LinkedIn? One way is that as you scroll through your feed, you will see a post and above it, it might read, "Knox Keith liked this post."

Another way is to look at someone's profile. When you do, you will see "Activity," which shows you their posts, comments, videos, documents, likes, etc. And, it tells you how long ago they were active.

As of this draft, looking at my own Activity section, I can see the following:

- For posts: my last two were eight hours ago (this morning) and yesterday.
- For comments: three minutes, three hours and one day.
- For videos: no date stamp, just thumbnails of all my videos.
- For images: again, no date stamp, just thumbnails of all my photos.
- For reactions (think Likes): 32 minutes, five hours, one day.

You can quickly see whether someone is leveraging LinkedIn or if it is an abandoned ghost town.

Why It Matters

Here are three reasons. First, part of my background is in sales, marketing, and communications. If I meet anyone related to these spaces, and they are not active on LinkedIn, then my first impression of them isn't great. They aren't taking advantage of the platform.

Second, there's a human-to-human (H2H) side of social media. Social media was not designed to broadcast information. It was designed to be a platform where people connect and have conversations (i.e., to be social). And, it tells me a lot about their mindset. Is that individual simply bragging about their accomplishments, or are they adding value to their network?

Third, have you ever noticed your own LinkedIn news feed? I just mentioned that as you scroll through it, you will find things that people in your network have posted and ads, of course. But LinkedIn will also put things in your newsfeed that your network has liked, even if you do not have a first-degree connection with the person whose post they liked.

That means that when you like someone's post, then you are amplifying their post to your network. Now, the algorithms are always changing, so there is not any perfect strategy for liking. Every time you do though, you tell your network that you found something valuable, and you help someone in your network get their message out.

Knox POV: While I do not have a formula or profess to know the intricacies of the every changing LinkedIn algorithm, I have witnessed a somewhat tiered system. That is, likes have a certain weight, but comments—especially those that are more thoughtful and engaging (versus as simple "Agreed!" or "Great post")—carry more weight in terms of visibility. The key is to be active on the platform.

Statistics

- Profiles that engage weekly receive five times more profile views and four times more connection requests than inactive accounts.

- Commenting on 15 posts per week can increase your reach by up to 300 percent as compared to posting alone.

"Participation in the new promotion."

—Jay Baer

Strategic Effects

Right now, we have been leaning into *analyze + act + repeat*, so I would be remiss if I didn't add that being active on the platform is where repeat matters most. If you want to stay visible, you have to show up consistently. Activity isn't a one-time tactic; it's a daily and weekly rhythm.

Mini Case Study

One of my clients landed a consulting gig not from a post but from a comment. She had commented thoughtfully on an industry leader's thread. Someone from a Fortune 500 saw it, checked her profile, and sent her a DM.

One comment turned into visibility that later turned into a contract.

Section 7—Experience (Job Descriptions)

Would you ever send out a resume without job descriptions in your experience / job history section? Of course not! Yet so many people choose not to include any descriptions in their LinkedIn profiles!

Why It Matters

Yes, you will continue to hear me say this: LinkedIn is not your resume. It's much, much more. But you must have one to three bullet points per job listed on LinkedIn.

Think of your LinkedIn Experience section as a movie trailer. You don't (and can't) tell your whole professional story in a trailer. A movie trailer is designed to spark interest and drive people to the theaters (or Netflix).

So give your LinkedIn audience enough snippets to spark that interest, so they reach out to you, just like the headhunter for Dell did with me.

Let's take a step back and review what a resume is or should be.

Rethinking the Resume

Let's start with something I've said before and will say again: LinkedIn is not your resume.

Most of us were handed the idea of a resume sometime in high school or college. A one-page document, perfectly formatted, that tells the world where we've worked and what we've done. It was supposed to be our golden ticket: our entry pass into jobs, internships and interviews. To some degree, it still plays that role.

But a resume is not your autobiography. It is not the complete narrative of your career, and it certainly shouldn't read like a laundry list of responsibilities.

Think of your resume as an *introduction.* Think of it more like advertising than documentation. It's a teaser. A glimpse. A quick scan of who you are professionally, what you bring to the table, and why you're worth a conversation. It's job is not to tell your whole story; it's to make someone want to know more.

If a resume is the movie trailer, your LinkedIn profile is the behind-the-scenes interview where you show your personality, talk about the making of your career, and invite people into a more human connection.

The Limits of the Resume

As we move through our careers, the resume becomes more limited, not more complete. Think about it: after 10, 15, or 25 years of working, no one's resume can effectively capture the nuance, evolution, or impact of their work without becoming a bloated, unreadable mess.

That's why LinkedIn offers something more dynamic. Your profile isn't bound by the same conventions. It allows for rich media, longer descriptions, personality, commentary, and *actual human tone.*

But let's not throw the resume under the bus just yet.

There's still value in knowing how to write one well and, more importantly, how to translate that understanding to your LinkedIn Experience section.

Resume vs. LinkedIn Experience

Here's the big difference:

- A resume is about *fit*. It's written to match a specific job description, optimized for keywords, and tailored to each opportunity.
- LinkedIn is about *validation*. It shows the arc of your professional journey, patterns of growth, and transferable strengths. It validates your credibility when someone Googles you. LinkedIn is the social proof for your career, and when used optimally, it builds your digital presence and validation to show who you are as a leader.

In other words, the resume is a pitch to HR or a hiring manager. LinkedIn is proof to the world.

What Belongs in the Experience Section?

This is the section where most people go wrong. Too often, I see the following:

- Company names and job titles with nothing in the job description.
- Paragraphs of dense text describing the company (not the professional responsibilities and accomplishments).

- Cliched and overused phrases:
  - "Results-oriented self-starter with cross-functional expertise in value-added synergies".
  - "Highly motivated".
  - "Passionate leader".

Please do not do the things above. You are better than this!

Given these limitations, you should give one to three focused, interesting, and skimmable bullet points for each role. The goal is to paint a picture of what you've accomplished, not just what your job was.

Remember, you have to think of your audience. Who is viewing your LinkedIn profile? Headhunters. Recruiters. Hiring managers. People you want to network with to gain exposure to new companies, opportunities, and referrals.

Stop limiting how you describe yourself. LinkedIn does not have to be all business all the time.

Instead, think more descriptively: What makes you interesting? What can you share that positions you as a go-getter? A leader? A team player? Someone who is responsible? Someone who takes action? Someone who is creative? Someone who is process oriented?

Whatever it is, this is your opportunity to create your own movie trailer, one that encourages them to click to connect. Or respond to your DM. Or forward your profile to their hiring department.

This is why I get incredibly frustrated when I see a LinkedIn profile for someone who has not bothered to even copy the words from their resume into their LinkedIn profile. They are shooting themselves in the foot and denying themselves an opportunity by choosing not to do the bare minimum. And the bare minimum, in my opinion, is a fully optimized LinkedIn presence.

So, what should you put in your Experience section?

Think in terms of competencies and accomplishments. Here's a simple structure I teach in my workshops:

1. Show the scope: Let the reader know the scale of your job and environment you worked in.

   "Led digital marketing efforts for a regional healthcare provider with 30+ clinics."

2. Describe the impact: Focus on outcomes, not duties.

   "Increased online appointment bookings by 48 percent through SEO and PPC optimization."

3. Highlight your competencies: What did this role demonstrate about your abilities? Leadership, strategy, collaboration, resilience?

   "Mentored and developed a team of five junior marketers, fostering a culture of ownership and accountability."

Not every bullet needs all three parts, but overall it should reflect them.

Oh, and please be interesting.

One of the most overlooked elements in writing job descriptions, whether on a resume or LinkedIn, is tone. That doesn't mean being cute or informal, but it does mean showing personality and specificity.

> "Responsible for managing budgets" is boring.
>
> "Managed a $4.2M annual budget and restructured vendor contracts to save $215K in one fiscal year" is not.

The goal here isn't to be verbose. It's to make your reader care. Hiring managers, recruiters, collaborators, and clients are scanning your profile to answer one question: Is this someone I want to know more about?

Do not bore them into skipping over you. Do not do things that make you blend into the crowd and become or stay invisible.

If you're a small business owner or entrepreneur, your Experience section isn't just background; it's proof of how you think about and build your business. It gives credibility to your journey and reassures potential partners, clients, or referrers that you know what you're doing.

Research shows that 78 percent of consumers discover new businesses through social media. That number climbs when the owner has a strong personal presence, especially on LinkedIn.

By showing up consistently, describing what you've built, and sharing how your responsibilities have evolved, you create awareness and trust. That's what moves people through your funnel, from being curious to becoming a client.

Tell the story of your business: how it grew, how you pivoted, what you've learned, and the value you bring.

Final Thought: Start with One Role

If this feels overwhelming, don't panic. Throughout this book we focus on the mindset of *crawl – walk – run*.

We are all starting at different points in our journey. So break down what you need to do just like we evolve: from crawling to walking to then running. It's a natural progression.

Pick your most recent (or most relevant) role, and update just that one. Use the format above. Make it human. Add bullet points. Focus on clarity and impact.

Then take a break and come back and do the next one when you're ready.

Your goal is not to impress people with how many jobs you've had or your job titles. Your job is to connect with the right ones by telling the parts of your story that matter most.

Remember, your resume might get you an interview, but your LinkedIn profile shows the world who you really are.

Wrapping Up the Experience Section

Follow these basic rules: Include one to three bullet points per job. Use keywords. Highlight outcomes.

What not to write:

- "Responsible for ____ tasks"
- Describing the *company*, not your role

How to make it better:

- "Launched new menu and increased dinner traffic by 23 percent in six months."

Your work experience should tell a story, not just be a list of job titles.

Statistics

- LinkedIn profiles with detailed work experience receive five times more connection requests and eight times more profile views than those with incomplete job descriptions.
- Recruiters are 44 percent more likely to contact candidates whose profiles list specific accomplishments vs. job duties.
- Job seekers with at least three bullet points per role are 27 percent more likely to receive InMail from recruiters.

"Your experience isn't just your history. It's proof of value."

—Amanda Russell

Strategic Effects

Experience is where analyze (what matters most from your story) meets act (how you present it):

This is where you move from observation to action. Your Experience section isn't about listing what happened; it's about shaping how the story is told.

Section 8—Contact Info & Other Sections

I created the Other sections to capture a few things that can easily help set you apart from your competition on LinkedIn. Yes, I said competition.

We often don't think of it as that, but one of your goals on LinkedIn is to position yourself in the best light. That way when you get compared to someone else, you shine more.

And if more than 80 percent of your competition is not doing these things, then this section will provide you with some very simple ways to help you stand out more and will give you examples of how to succeed.

Why It Matters

These often-overlooked pieces of your fully optimized LinkedIn presence is where your profile moves from one-dimensional to three-dimensional. Where you humanize your brand. Where you find ways to connect with other people.

Let's start off with another thing that drives me absolutely crazy: your contact information.

Would you ever send out a resume without an email address or phone number? Hell no! So why do people ignore this on LinkedIn?

I recommend putting your contact information in two places. The obvious one is Contact Information. Provide at least one of the two: email address or phone number. The second place is in your About section.

I know, I know. There's so much spam these days. Generally we have more than one email account, so if you're afraid of too much spam, provide one of your secondary accounts. Just be sure to check it on a regular basis.

Phone numbers can feel more invasive, so I recommend setting up a Google number.

The key here is that if a recruiter or hiring manager is interested in you, they need to be able to reach you! I wound up with an unadvertised opportunity with Dell because I was visible on social media (that is, I was sharing good stuff and adding value) and because the headhunter had a way to contact me.

So why do I recommend adding your contact info in two places? Well, your contact info might be hidden based on the number of degrees of separation or privacy settings. I recommend also putting it in your About section to remove this obstacle.

Other Sections

There are many other smaller sections or information that you can add to help set you apart from others and validate who you are professionally.

- Volunteer work / charities

  Why It Matters: You never know how you might connect with a decision maker, so avoid writing that you are "passionate about animals." Instead, link to the SPCA group, and describe the volunteer work you did with them. This fits my mantra of *show, don't tell.* Plus, visually it's more impactful because their logo will show up on your profile.

- Hobbies

  Why It Matters: Again, you never know how you might connect with a decision maker.

  Case Study 1: I attended college in the 1980s when it seemed like everyone went on to attend law school. I thought I should get a job at a law firm to show my interest in that industry, but in a college town, those jobs were hard to come by. On my resume, one of my hobbies was softball. Turns out the firm where I interviewed and later was hired was in need of more players for its company softball team.

Case Study 2: A daughter of a friend of mine was applying to residency programs coming out of medical school. For the Texas-based schools, her father encouraged her to list skeet shooting. While this hobby may not have played well in every state, he insisted that it would make a difference. Reluctantly, she added it.

After the interview process, she shared with her father that the interviewers were avid skeet shooters and that they spent the majority of the interview discussing shotguns and bird hunting. And later, she received a residency with that school.

Why? Because the hobby was a point of connection. People want to work with people with whom they have something in common. It's that human to human element that we've discussed previously.

Currently, though, LinkedIn does not have a hobby section. If you have an interesting hobby, I encourage you to add it to your About section.

- Featured and Projects

  Why It Matters: Are you noticing a theme with this section? Actually, this is two sections as LinkedIn offers both a Featured section and a Projects section. It is the same point though. Showcasing some of your work helps round out who you are on LinkedIn and adds an element to your digital footprint that a resume alone could never do. So take advantage of it!

- Recommendations

  Why It Matters: Recommendations are third-party proof points. They validate your skills, credibility, and the impact you've had on others in a way that no self-written headline or bullet point ever can. Strong recommendations shift your profile from "Trust me" to "Here's the evidence." They provide social proof that builds confidence in your professional brand, echoing my mantra of *show, don't tell.* Recruiters, clients, and decision-makers read them because they want to see how others describe working with you, not just how you describe yourself.

Case Study 3: One of my MBA students was interviewing for a competitive consulting role. Her resume and GPA were solid, but what ultimately tipped the scales was a glowing LinkedIn recommendation from a senior executive for whom she had interned. During the interview, the hiring manager mentioned the recommendation by name and said, "If someone like that speaks this highly of you, we know you can deliver." That single paragraph of praise carried more weight than pages of bullet points.

Quick Win: Ask one colleague or client for a recommendation this week. One strong testimonial can outweigh a dozen bullet points.

Statistics

- Profiles with clearly visible contact information receive 35 percent more inbound outreach from recruiters and hiring managers.
- 62 percent of recruiters say they move on to the next candidate if they can't find a way to contact someone directly.
- Profiles with volunteer experience get six times more views than those without.
- 77 percent of hiring managers say shared interests can positively influence their perception of a candidate.
- Profiles that use LinkedIn's Featured section see 2.3 times more engagement on average.
- Projects and media-rich elements increase time spent on profile by 45 seconds per visitor.
- Candidates with at least one recommendation are three times more likely to be contacted by recruiters.
- People trust peer endorsements two times more than self-promotion.

Outside Perspective

"What others say about you is infinitely more powerful than what you say about yourself."

—Jay Baer

Mini Case Study: Jonathan—Turning Credibility into Proof

Jonathan had been in his industry for 15 years, but his LinkedIn profile looked like it belonged to someone in year one. No Featured section. No recommendations. No activity. No real signal of trust.

We started small. We optimized his profile. He reached out to three former colleagues with a simple, specific request for a recommendation. Within two weeks, his profile shifted from flat to credible. The recommendations told the story he never had to brag about.

Key Takeaway

Let other people do the bragging for you. Social proof builds trust fast.

Final Thought: You Are a Professional Brand and the Face of Your Brand

We have just walked through the nuts and bolts of optimizing your LinkedIn profile from your headline to your recommendations and everything in between. That may feel like a lot of detail, but each piece adds up to one powerful message: your credibility.

If you're a small business owner, executive, or professional, you may not want to be the face of your brand. But the truth is, you already are.

People connect with people. Your profile is your 24/7 digital storefront, and it speaks before you even walk into the room.

Your LinkedIn presence doesn't have to be perfect; it just has to be complete, real, and intentional. When you put in the effort, opportunities begin to find you instead of the other way around.

Let's stop giving your LinkedIn presence a ghost-town energy. You just have to show up and be seen.

Next up? We'll move beyond the profile and into your content strategy, the engine that keeps your brand visible, trusted, and top-of-mind.

QR Code

CHAPTER 8
Purpose of Content

In Chapters 6 and 7 we optimized our presence on LinkedIn, so we can present a strong, professional presence and make a good first impression.

Now we are going to do a deeper dive on what to share and how to position yourself as a subject matter expert, thought leader, and go-to resource.

Your Content Has a Job to Do

The first thing that your content should do is to add value—not to you but to your network.

Amanda Russell, author of *The Influencer Code*, states, "Influence is the ability to get someone to take action." In order to do that, you must have awareness + trust + benevolence. Benevolence is demonstrated by adding value to your network through your posts and your content.

This is contrary to the popular theory that all you need is awareness or visibility. Visibility without credibility is just noise, or things that we do not pay attention to.

Visibility is not the same as credibility.

Credibility is built by showing up consistently over time, expressing your point of view, and adding value in your posts and comments.

Credibility is what moves someone through the sales funnel (awareness – consideration – purchase) from awareness to consideration.

You can be visible and still not be *valued*. You can post daily and still be *ignored*. Visibility can get you into the room, but credibility is what makes people want to *listen*.

Knox POV: Social media isn't social if all you do is broadcast. *Social* means that you are engaging—having conversations with people—versus just posting stuff.

Statistics

- 80 percent of your visibility on LinkedIn comes from engagement, not posts. (More on engagement in Chapter 12.)
- Posts that spark a conversation generate on average two times more reach than promotional posts.
- Professionals who post once per week are 10 times more likely to be contacted for new opportunities.
- Human stories outperform corporate speak. Personal and behind-the-scenes content can increase engagement by 30–50 percent as compared to purely promotional content.

Back to Content

Social media wasn't built to be a one-way megaphone.

It was designed to be social: two-way, conversational, and engaging. That means your content should not be limited to just stating things. It should invite connection and conversation.

Too many professionals (and too many influencers) treat LinkedIn like it's a radio station. Just announcements and achievements. Promotions and reposts. That's broadcasting. It's not social!

Real professionals build trust through content that sparks conversation. The right content demonstrates how they think, what they value, and who they help.

Knox POV:

> *"The power of social media lies in the conversations."*

And conversations begin with content that serves a purpose.

The Eight Purposes of Content

In this chapter we will take a deeper look at each of these purposes. Please note, these are in no particular order:

1. Inform / Educate
2. Motivate / Inspire
3. Humanize / Connect
4. Position / Lead
5. Recognize / Reward
6. Entertain / Delight
7. Engage / Converse
8. Promote / Brag

Knox POV:

"If your content doesn't have a purpose, it doesn't belong in your feed. Period."

Every post should have a job. A purpose. A reason to exist. If it doesn't, don't publish it. I call this the *So what? factor*. As in, "So, what's the purpose of this post?" Does it help someone? Does it add value? Does it position a product, service, company, event, or myself in a better light?

Let's explore each purpose.

Inform / Educate

Use your content to teach. Share industry tips, how-to guides, product insights, or frameworks.

Give your audience something that adds to their toolkit.

When I post tips on content atomization or process improvement, I'm not selling. I'm providing value. Education builds authority or subject matter expertise.

Mini Case Study

I once shared a short post breaking down how to "atomize" one long blog post into seven LinkedIn posts. It wasn't flashy, just useful. That single post generated more than 20 DMs from people asking for templates and strategy help.

Educational content builds credibility fast because it gives people something they can use immediately.

Motivate / Inspire

Sometimes your audience needs fuel, not just facts. Share a quote that made you pause and why or how it made you pause.

Share a challenge you've overcome or a moment that mattered. Posts of this nature can help you connect with others.

I often use #MotivationalMonday, not to preach but to reflect. The best inspiration is honest, not performative.

Mini Case Study

When I shared a personal post about getting back to fitness and doing Tough Mudder races after turning 40 and getting divorced, I wasn't trying to motivate anyone. But it resonated. Dozens of people commented or DM'd their own comeback stories.

Real, vulnerable reflection often inspires people far more than polished "inspirational" quotes ever could.

Humanize / Connect

This is where you become a real person, not just a resume. Show a behind-the-scenes moment. Highlight your team. Share a photo from a volunteering event with context.

My posts from conferences or charity events tend to perform well, not because they're flashy but because they're *real.* People connect with people. (Remember it's not business to business or business to consumer. instead it's human to human. People do business with other people.)

Mini Case Study

After posting a photo from my trip to Normandy with a short reflection on D-Day, I heard from former colleagues and complete strangers alike. The post wasn't about business, but it built connections.

Human moments remind people you're a person, not just a title.

Position / Lead

Share your perspective in a way that adds value to the conversation. Don't just repost articles. Explain why they matter to your industry, clients, or peers.

This is real thought leadership. It's about clarity, not ego. It shows how you process trends and connect them back to meaningful outcomes.

For example, when new technologies or practices emerge, you can frame them in context: how they augment work, improve efficiency, or create risks instead of as wholesale replacements for human judgment. This kind of framing positions you as someone who understands the landscape and can help others navigate it.

Mini Case Study

Years ago, when a major platform changed how it handled e-commerce integrations, I posted my POV on what it meant for marketers and operators. By adding my POV with relevant context, it opened up meaningful dialogue and positioned me as someone who could help others navigate the change.

Real thought leadership adds signal and direction.

Recognize / Reward

Shine a light on others. Celebrate teammates, peers, or clients. Recognition isn't just kind; it's strategic. It tells your network you're collaborative and generous. It *shows* instead of tells.

I've seen better engagement from one shout-out post than from 10 self-promotional ones.

Mini Case Study

I once posted a public thank-you to a client team after a big launch, highlighting *their* work, not mine. That one post outperformed my other content three to one.

Recognition builds goodwill and amplifies your reach.

Entertain / Delight

It's okay to have a little fun. Polls, surveys, memes (used appropriately), or behind-the-scenes moments can drive powerful engagement.

For me, polls have been a goldmine. Some of them are entertaining. They invite interaction and show I'm listening.

Mini Case Study: Taco Tuesday

My #TacoTuesday posts started as something fun and personal. Over time, they became a conversation starter and a subtle trust builder. People started sending me taco memes and sometimes those conversations led to new opportunities.

That's the power of content that delights: It connects in a human way and sticks.

Engage / Converse

Start a conversation. Ask questions. Respond to others. Don't just post; participate!

When you ask thoughtful questions on other people's posts or invite dialogue on your own, you turn scrolling into connection. Conversations are content, and they build trust faster than one-way broadcasts ever could.

Mini Case Study: Ted Sockies

One of Ted's most engaged posts wasn't a big campaign; it was a pair of crazy socks. Ted's Sockies sparked hundreds of comments and conversations, and even its own hashtag!

The magic wasn't in the socks. It was in the story and how it invited others to share their own.

Promote / Brag (10 Percent)

Yes, you can sell and should sell yourself. Just don't make it all you do. Share testimonials, launches, and awards—just keep it in balance.

If 90 percent of your content serves others, the 10 percent that promotes *you* will be earned.

Case in Point: Small Things, Big Ripples

A pair of socks. A taco post. Neither was a master marketing plan. But both started conversations, created connections, and led to business.

> *"Sometimes, your best-performing content isn't the most strategic; it's the most human."*
>
> —Knox

Why It Matters

Inform / Educate

Knowledge builds credibility. When you share useful insights, people begin to see you as a trusted resource, not just another voice online.

Motivate / Inspire

Inspiration fuels action. A motivating post can spark energy, hope, or focus in others, and they'll remember you as the source of that spark.

Humanize / Connect

People connect with people, not logos. Sharing authentic stories and experiences makes you relatable, approachable, and memorable.

Position / Lead

Thought leadership is about clarity, not ego. By adding your perspective, you show how you think and help others make sense of trends and change.

Recognize / Reward

Recognition creates community. When you spotlight others, you build goodwill, strengthen relationships, and expand your reach.

Entertain / Delight

Delight makes people lean in. Humor, surprise, or joy breaks through the noise and makes your content worth sharing.

Engage / Converse

Engagement drives relationships. When you start conversations instead of broadcasting, you create dialogue that deepens trust and expands your influence.

Promote / Brag

If you don't tell your story, no one else will. Sharing wins and milestones builds proof, credibility, and momentum for your brand.

Jay Baer, *Author of Talk Triggers*:

"Content that gets talked about is rarely the loudest; it's the most useful, delightful, or surprising."

Knox POV: I love this quote because it captures what most people get wrong about content. It's not about volume. It's not about you. It's about resonance.

The posts that travel the farthest aren't the ones yelling the loudest; they are the ones that make people feel something, learn something, or smile. That's why purpose matters so much. If your content earns attention instead of demanding it, it creates conversation. And conversation is where credibility grows.

"The personal brand that wins isn't the one with the most followers; it's the one that consistently shows up with purpose and generosity."

—Mark Schaefer, Author of *Known*

Knox POV: This is the heartbeat of everything I teach. Visibility means nothing if it isn't backed by credibility. A smaller, engaged audience that trusts you will always outperform a larger one that doesn't care. Purpose and generosity compound over time. They build authority, trust, and opportunity. That's what Digital Validatio™ is built on: showing up with intention, not just showing up.

Credibility Comes from Purpose

Every piece of content that you create should reflect at least one of the purposes above. Not all at once. Not always perfectly. But always with intention.

This is the difference between content that performs and sticks and content that fades into the background.

When your content consistently adds value by educating, connecting, or inspiring, you stop chasing opportunities. Opportunities start finding you.

Knox POV:

"People don't chase value. They're drawn to it."

Your audience will begin to associate your name with a specific set of ideas. That's credibility. That's positioning.

That's Digital Validation™

Tying Content to Strategic Effects in Action

Let's overlay my Strategic Effects framework that I introduced earlier in the book with your evaluation of your content:

- **Awareness**: Are you showing up regularly with relevant content?

  Consistency signals that you're present, credible, and part of the conversation. If you're silent, then you're invisible.

  Question: How often does your network see you adding value?

- **Orientation**: Are you helping your audience understand who you are and what you offer?

  Content should give people a clear sense of your role, expertise, and values. If someone binge-read your last 10 posts, would they "get" you?

  Question: What picture would they paint of you today?

- **Decision**: Are you demonstrating credibility, so others choose to follow, connect, or work with you?

  People make micro-decisions every day about who to trust, who to connect with, and who to hire. Proof points in your content (case studies, lessons learned, or recognition of others) help tip those scales.

  Question: Are you giving people enough reasons to believe in you?

- **Action**: Are your posts encouraging conversations, shares, DMs, or opportunities?

Engagement is the bridge from visibility to relationships. Strong content doesn't just inform; it sparks interaction that can lead to business, collaborations, or career growth.

Question: When was the last time content you shared led to a real-world opportunity?

When your content serves a clear purpose, each post plays a role in moving someone through this path. That's when content stops being random marketing and becomes intentional and strategy.

15 Rules for Creating Great Content

As we create content, we need to abide by some rules:

1. *Share good stuff.*

   Add value. Be helpful. Limit the fluff. If people associate your posts with insights that matter, they'll keep coming back for more.

2. *Do not overshare.*

   This is LinkedIn, not Facebook. Keep the birthday drama, family feuds, and personal oversharing off your professional brand.

3. *You do not need to start from scratch.*

   Curate. You're already reading great articles, so share them with your own perspective on why they matter. That's value creation without reinventing the wheel.

4. *Stick to your content pillars.*

   Consistency builds recognition. If your audience can't connect you with specific themes, you'll blend into the noise.

5. *Be transparent.*

   Let people know who you are, what you do, and why you care. At Dell, employees tagged posts with #DellEmployee, a small but powerful way to ensure transparency.

6. *Protect sensitive information.*

   Guard what's not yours to share. Never post confidential details like financial results, customer information, product roadmaps, or internal strategies. Protecting information protects your credibility, too.

7. *Do not feed the trolls.*

   Negativity thrives on attention. Responding to trolls only amplifies them. Ignore or block them, and move on.

8. *Do not speak ill of your competitors.*

   Criticism cheapens your brand. Instead, differentiate by showing your strengths and values. People respect leaders who rise above negativity.

9. *Give credit where credit is due.*

   Always attribute ideas, quotes, or content you share. Tag the author, link the source, and highlight others. It builds trust and community.

10. *Avoid clickbait.*

    Catchy headlines are fine; misleading ones are not. Credibility dies when people feel tricked. Your reputation is more valuable than a one-time spike in views.

11. *Respect your audience's time.*

    Attention is a gift. Keep your posts clear, focused, and to the point. Shorter, sharper posts are more likely to be read, remembered, and acted on.

12. *Don't chase virality.*

    Virality is a lottery, not a strategy. Focus instead on creating consistent, useful content that steadily builds your reputation and reach.

13. *Keep it professional.*

    You do not have to be buttoned-up all the time, but you should always be intentional. Let your personality come through in ways that reinforce your professional image.

14. *Encourage dialogue; don't preach.*

    Posts that spark conversations create more impact than one-way broadcasts. Ask questions, invite perspectives, and keep the discussion alive.

15. *Be human.*

    Professional does not mean robotic. AI can feel inauthentic. Show empathy, humor, and humanity. People want to connect with people, not job titles. #HumanToHuman or #H2H

Exercise

What Should You Be Posting?

Go back to the last 10 posts that you've made. Categorize them under one of the eight purposes of content.

Use this moment to reset:

- Choose two to three primary content purposes that align with your goals.
- Draft (and schedule) three new post ideas using those purposes as you filter.

Show, Don't Tell

If you have to *say* that you are a leader, you're probably not showing us that you are. Instead of telling people that you're a great coach, show them with content that educates.

Proof is more powerful than proclamations.

Sometimes Something Random Can Stick

Remember my taco obsession? That started off as a one-off #TacoTuesday post, and it clicked, so much so that several years ago, McCormick's Spices had an open position for Director of taco relations. An astonishing 72 of my contacts, including former clients, emailed or DM'd me the link to apply for that job!

Instead of outbound marketing efforts, the taco theme (err, obsession) has led to people sending me taco memes: *Hey Knox, I saw this Taco Tuesday meme, and it reminded me of you. Oh, by the way, we are currently experiencing something where we could use your help. Do you have time to whiteboard it with us in the next couple of weeks?*

This has led to at least a quarter of a million dollars' worth of business for me over the years! Why? Because my love for all things tacos is *real.* And in a world of generic and AI-generated profiles, a little personality goes a long way.

Final Thoughts

Content isn't a filler. It's not busy work. It's not something you do just because your marketing team says you should.

Content is how you shape perception. It's how you build authority. It's how you start conversations and earn trust.

Visibility will get you noticed.

But content with purpose, intentionality, and consistency is what gets you seen.

In Chapter 8, we will use all of the previous work to build our professional personas.

"Our data shows that engagement—thoughtful comments, reposts with context, and meaningful conversations—drives professional opportunity more than follower counts or flashy content."

—LinkedIn CEO Ryan Roslansky (2023)

QR Code

CHAPTER 9
Develop Your Persona—Think Like a Publicist

In Chapter 8, we learned the purposes of content. In Chapter 9, we will start to frame your professional self and learn how to think like a publicist for getting your story and reputation out into the world. In Chapter 10, we will build your content framework.

Congratulations! You've Been Promoted!

I know it's not always a great feeling when your boss adds more to your already-full plate. Nonetheless, congratulations are in order! You're no longer just a professional in your field. You're now your own publicist.

Your job is to manage and shape how the world sees you online. It's not about chasing attention or becoming an influencer; it's about being intentional with your presence and showcasing the value you bring professionally.

The good news? You have all the raw material. Now it's time to organize it.

What Is a Persona?

A professional persona is your digital posture: how you present yourself in a way that reflects your experience, values, tone, and expertise. It's how you show up, consistently and credibly.

Think of it as a curated version of your real self, tailored for a professional audience.

Unlike personal branding, which often gets confused with selfies, slogans, and a mindset of "Look at me, I'm important," your professional persona is grounded in substance. It shows, rather than tells, who you are.

Why It Matters

Your professional persona influences how others perceive your credibility and your expertise. It is your digital reputation.

It builds trust, fosters connection, and can open doors you didn't know existed. When done right, your professional persona is the foundation of your Digital Validation™.

Strategic Effects

In the Strategic Effects framework, defining your persona is part analyze (understanding how you want to be seen) and part act (intentionally showing up that way). If you do not define it, others will define it for you. A strong professional persona lets you take control of the narrative before anyone else writes it for you. Additionally, defining and supporting your persona helps you become strategic and intentional about what people find about you.

Outside Perspective

"The personal brand that wins isn't the one with the most followers; it's the one that consistently shows up with purpose and generosity."

—Mark Schaefer, Author of *Known*

This is the real power of a strong persona. It's not about going viral or chasing a big audience. It is about showing up in a way that's consistent, clear, and purposeful. When you show up consistently, you build credibility and trust. This will build your Digital Validation™, and people will start to pay attention.

Generosity builds connection. Purpose builds trust. And together, they create a presence that cuts through the noise, even if you don't have the biggest following.

The Anatomy of a Persona

To build a strong persona, you need to map out both your professional and personal storylines.

1. Baseline Persona (Old School / Limited Mindset)

Most professionals stop at the baseline. They build their persona like a resume:

- Job title and employer
- Education and certifications
- Departments and industries worked in
- Promotions and responsibilities
- KPIs and accomplishments

This is fine. It's safe, but it's also flat. There's no sense of connection. A baseline business persona tells people *what* you've done without telling them *who* you are or *why* you matter. On LinkedIn, that's not enough to stand out.

Remember, people want to connect with people, so you're going to have to open up a little bit more to stand out and become multidimensional.

2. Multidimensional Persona (Modern Mindset)

A stronger persona goes beyond static labels. It creates *connection + credibility* by showing your professional expertise *and* your human touch.

Professional Core

- What themes of expertise define your work?
- Which industries, roles, or outcomes give you credibility?

Personal Touchpoints

- What interests, experiences, or causes make you relatable?
- What milestones, travels, or challenges shaped you?

Values, Voice, and Vibe

- **Values:** What principles guide you?
- **Voice:** What tone do you naturally bring?
- **Vibe:** How do others feel after engaging with you?

Your Professional Persona = Expertise + Human Touch + Signal

1. Expertise

The credibility piece—your knowledge, roles, industries, and measurable results—are what make people trust that you know your stuff.

2. Human Touch

The relatability piece—your stories, hobbies, values, quirks, and lived experiences—are what make people feel connected to you as a person, not just a title.

3. Signal

The expression piece—how you project your persona outwardly into the digital world—is what turns your expertise and humanity into a clear, consistent professional presence that others can immediately identify and trust.

- Your *voice* (tone of your content, how you write, and how you comment).
- Your *vibe* (the emotions people feel after engaging with you: inspired, motivated, challenged, etc.).
- Your *consistency* (showing up in the same authentic way across LinkedIn posts, comments, About section, and even offline conversations).

Signal is the opposite of noise. It's the clear message people pick up about who you are and what you stand for. It answers the question: *What impression do I consistently leave behind?*

So, rephrased for clarity:

> *Persona = expertise (what you know) + human touch (who you are) + signal (how you show up and are experienced by others).*

The Persona Triangle

Your professional persona is strongest when it's built on three balanced points:

- **Expertise:** The foundation of credibility.
- **Human Touch:** The spark of connection.
- **Signal:** The outward expression that amplifies both.

Here's what happens when any one of these is missing:

- Expertise without human touch feels cold.
- Human touch without signal gets lost in the noise.
- Signal without substance comes off as performative.

A strong persona lives at the intersection of all three. That's where trust and opportunity meet.

Pro Tip: Download and print *The Persona Triangle* from the QR Code, and keep it visible as you build your digital presence. It's not just a model; it's your positioning filter.

Outside Perspective

"A strong persona isn't about putting on a mask; it's about putting your best story forward. Publicists don't invent who you are; they help shape how the world experiences you. That's exactly what your online persona should do: give people something clear, human, and memorable to hold on to."

—Alek Irvin, PR Strategist

Show-Don't-Tell Moment

I once commented on a post about leadership frameworks—not promoting myself, just offering a clear, thoughtful point of view. Within 48 hours, two people DM'd me regarding consulting opportunities. That's a signal in action: Your voice creates opportunities when it reflects your persona.

Mini Case Studies

Your persona is your signal, and when it's clear, it creates momentum. I've seen it happen again and again with founders, mid-career leaders, and students just starting out. Here are three composite stories that reflect the patterns I've witnessed firsthand.

Mini Case Study #1: Small Business Owner—From Hidden to Seen

Over the years, I've worked with a lot of small business owners who fall into the same trap: They're excellent at what they do but almost invisible online.

One of them, Sonia, ran a thriving boutique financial planning firm. Her LinkedIn presence was bare bones: title, certifications, and bullet points. That was it. No story. No signal.

Once she defined her persona and became active on LinkedIn, things changed. Sonia started weaving in short, thoughtful posts about why she became a financial planner: to help small business owners build freedom and legacy.

She shared client wins (with permission), personal insights, and a few glimpses of her love for gardening and mentoring young women.

Within three months, the tone of her inbound messages shifted. Instead of sending cold DMs, she received warm, qualified inquiries. People often said, *"I feel like I already know you."*

Key Takeaway

When your persona reflects your values and passions, people don't just see your skills; they trust your story. They connect with you.

Mini Case Study #2: Mid-Career Professional—From Forgettable to Top of Mind

I see this often with mid-career professionals: years of solid experience but an online presence that reads like a resume, not a narrative. Marcus is a composite of several operations leaders I've coached.

On paper, Marcus was impressive: 15 years in supply chain and operations. But his persona and presence were flat. No voice. No angle. Just titles and dates.

After working through his persona, he reframed his About section to highlight not only what he did, but *why* he did it: to build systems that make work easier, not harder, for the people on the front lines.

He began posting monthly reflections on leadership lessons, weaving in stories from the warehouse floor to the boardroom. He also shared moments from volunteering with youth sports, which humanized his professional image.

Within 10 weeks, he was contacted by multiple recruiters who said, "*Your profile feels like a conversation, not a job description.*"

Key Takeaway

A clear persona builds the kind of familiarity that gets you called before the job gets posted.

Mini Case Study #3: Early-Career Professional—From Unclear to Undeniable

I've seen this pattern dozens of times with early-career professionals and grad students. Jacob, a composite of several MBA students I've taught, had a technically strong profile: pre-MBA Fortune 500 experience, summer internship between his first and second year, and numerous leadership roles. But there was no continuity or theme. He was impressive but not memorable.

Once Jacob defined his persona, *"an intellectually curious problem-solver who connects business strategy and design,"* everything clicked. He reworked his profile to emphasize that theme, started sharing reflections from his job search and posted light, human content about what he was learning along the way.

One honest post about imposter syndrome received more engagement than his entire resume ever had. Hiring managers and recruiters began reaching out directly.

Key Takeaway

A well-defined persona gives even early-career professionals a powerful voice in crowded spaces.

Example: Knox's Persona

Here's what this looks like when I put it into practice:

Professional Core

- President of Knox Management Consulting.
- BA in English, MBA in Finance, with international coursework in Spain and England.
- Industries: manufacturing, high-tech, retail, oil & gas, education.

- Functions: consulting, marketing, sales, operations
- Managed $1bn e-commerce product line, led 87 direct reports
- Course creator and adjunct professor (trained 10,000-plus professionals)

Personal Touchpoints

- Emmy-winning storyteller
- Father of two (both creative, global thinkers)
- Traveler and photographer
- Taco aficionado and proud Texan

Values, Voice, and Vibe

- Values: integrity, connection, curiosity, challenging the status quo
- Voice: conversational, direct, motivating
- Vibe: inspiring, empowering, action-oriented

Notice how this shifts me from "consultant with an MBA" (baseline) to "trusted advisor, storyteller, and connector" (multidimensional).

Translating Your Persona into Your LinkedIn About Section

Sample Narrative / Intro Text

It's one thing to know who you are. It's another to make that clear online.

Your persona shouldn't live in a notebook or a worksheet. It should be reflected everywhere people might find you.

On LinkedIn, your About section is one of the most powerful places to make your persona visible. It's where you can weave your expertise, human touch, and signal into a short, memorable narrative.

Here's a simple way to bring it to life, moving from a raw persona to polished on LinkedIn.

Raw Persona Statement:

"I'm a mid-career marketing strategist with experience in retail and e-commerce. I love simplifying complex problems and helping teams grow. I'm also a huge foodie and enjoy traveling."

Good Persona Statement:

"I'm a marketing strategist with more than 15 years of experience in retail and e-commerce. I focus on solving complex marketing challenges and helping teams execute efficiently. I'm passionate about what I do and always looking for ways to grow."

- Professional but ...
- Generic. This reads like 90 percent of LinkedIn profiles. It tells but doesn't show.

Better Persona Statement:

"I help brands turn messy marketing into meaningful strategy. Over the last 15 years, I've led campaigns that scaled e-commerce businesses, modernized legacy retail, and grew teams from five to 50.

I'm most energized when I'm simplifying complexity, connecting dots others don't see and building strategies that work in the real world.

Outside of work, you'll find me exploring new cities, chasing great food, and collecting stories along the way. I believe relationships drive results on the ground and online."

- Keeps the expertise.
- Weaves in voice + vibe.
- Adds human touch.
- Shows what makes this person *different.*

Key Takeaway

Your persona gives you the raw ingredients. How you show up on LinkedIn turns those ingredients into a signature dish.

Common Myths About Building a Persona

As soon as you start defining your persona, it's normal for a few objections to bubble up. Let's clear those out before they slow you down.

- *"But I don't want to brag."*

  Your persona is not ego. It's clarity. You are not inflating your story. You're simply making it easier for others to understand your value.

- *"I'm not good at talking about myself."*

  That's why we use structure and storytelling. A clear persona gives you language and shape, so you don't have to wing it.

- *"I don't want to overshare."*

  LinkedIn and your personal story is not about sharing all your dirty laundry or making confessions. It's about curation. You choose the stories that build trust, not the ones that drain it.

These concerns don't mean you're doing it wrong; they mean you're human. Everyone wrestles with these questions. The difference is that the people who lean into clarity, not perfection, are the ones who get noticed.

The Strategy of Sharing

Once your persona is defined, it becomes the foundation of your content strategy.

It helps you determine the following:

- What topics you should consistently post about.
- How you engage in comments.
- What tone your audience expects from you.

This is not about oversharing. It's about showing up with clarity and intention.

Think of your persona as a filter. Every time you consider posting something, ask yourself these questions:

- Does this align with my core expertise?
- Does it reveal something human and relatable?
- Does it reinforce my values, voice, and vibe?

If the answers are yes, then it's on brand.

Common Mistakes to Avoid

Most people make one of two mistakes when building a persona:

1. Too narrow: They only list their title or employer. The result: one-dimensional and forgettable.
2. Too scattered: They share everything without a filter. The result: confusing and inconsistent.

The sweet spot is a curated mix: professional credibility + personal humanity.

Exercise: Frame Your Persona

Use the following prompts to build your own persona. Don't overthink it. Just brainstorm. You can refine later.

1. What is your current role? What are your daily responsibilities?
2. What is your educational background?
3. In what industries have you worked?
4. What are your proudest professional accomplishments?
5. What values define your leadership or approach?
6. What are your hobbies or interests?
7. What's a personal story that shaped who you are today?
8. What do you want people to say about you when you're not in the room?

Wrap up with a statement: "*I am…*"

(You can use this to enhance your LinkedIn About section or your personal pitch.)

The "Publicist Mindset"

If you were your own publicist (and you are!), how would you position yourself?

Draft your professional publicist plan:

- What do I want to be known for?
- How can I prove I know my stuff?
- What two to three places should I show up regularly online?
- Who in my network can I collaborate with?

This mindset forces you to step outside of your own head. A publicist wouldn't just recite your title. They'd highlight your credibility, personality, and proof points in a way that earns attention.

Jenna Soard's Twist: Theme + Litmus Test

Brand strategist Jenna Soard teaches that your brand should feel like a *character* with a theme, not just a resume.

Let's adapt some of her methods for LinkedIn personas.

Persona Theme Statement

Write a short sentence that captures your persona's essence:

- "I'm the bold-but-relatable challenger: I simplify complexity, question the status quo, and make people feel capable of more."

Litmus Test for Your Persona

Before posting something, ask yourself the following:

1. Does this align with my values?
2. Does this sound like my authentic voice?
3. Does this contribute to how I want to be seen in my industry?

If yes, then it passes. If no, then it's time to rethink it.

Parent Brand vs. Sub-Brands

- Parent = you (the whole person, multidimensional).
- Sub-brands = your roles, side hustles, or causes.

Final Thought

You are not your resume. You are not your job title. You are a whole person with depth, value, and a unique story to share.

Digital Validation™ begins by understanding who you are, how you want to be seen, and why it matters.

So go ahead. Step into the career role that you want to have. Embrace being your own publicist. And remember, the best way to stand out is to show up consistently, clearly, and with intention.

Key Takeaways

- Your persona is the bridge between who you are and how the world perceives you.
- If you don't define your signal, you will show up as just more noise.
- Expertise earns trust. Humanity builds connection. Signal drives opportunity.

QR Code

CHAPTER 10
Build Your Content Framework

Introduction: Stepping Back from the Ledge

One of the most common things I hear is this:

"I want to be more visible online, but I have no idea what to post."

If that's you, take a breath. This is not about becoming a full-time content creator. You do not need a fancy content calendar, a team of writers, or daily posts.

You just need a structure, a framework that helps you decide the following:

- What to talk about.
- What to share.
- How to show up consistently without burning out.

That structure is your content framework, content pillars, or content strategy. I tend to use those terms interchangeably.

This chapter is not about turning you into a marketing machine. It is about making content feel doable and repeatable.

Here's what's possible when you know your pillars:

- You can share a smart article and add a one-line POV.
- You can talk about a project you worked on.
- You can respond thoughtfully to an industry trend.

None of that requires hours of planning. It just requires clarity about what you stand for and what you want to be known for.

This is how professionals build visibility without adding a second job to their lives.

Why It Matters

When someone lands on your LinkedIn profile or sees your name in their feed, they should walk away with a clear sense of who you are, what you do, and what you care about. If your activity is scattered, silent, or inconsistent, they won't know what to make of you. When that happens, it means missed opportunities.

A content framework gives you these:

- A clear reputation roadmap so your presence is intentional, not accidental.
- A simple system to show up without overthinking every post.

- A way to build trust and authority over time through repetition and relevance.

Remember:

"You don't need to go viral.
You just need to show up and add value."

—Knox

So if visibility is not about going viral, what is it about? The answer is *clarity*. And clarity starts with your content pillars.

Outside Perspective: James Clear—Systems vs. Goals

In his book, *Atomic Habits*, James Clear says:

"You do not rise to the level of your goals. You fall to the level of your systems."

A content framework *is* your system. It keeps you consistent when inspiration dips, when work gets busy, and when your calendar feels full.

Key Takeaway

Systems make visibility sustainable.

How We Got Here

Let's review: In Chapter 8, we learned the purposes of content. In Chapter 9, we started thinking like a publicist. In Chapter 10, we will start to put it all together as we outline your Content Framework. Chapters 8 and 9 were light on exercises, which was needed after Chapters 6 and 7! Get ready to roll your sleeves up to do some more heavy lifting in Chapter 10.

Mini Case Study: From Uncertain to Intentional

One of my MBA students came to me frustrated. She said, "*I never know what to post, so I end up posting nothing.*"

We worked together to build her content framework: five professional pillars, one personal, and one cause she cared about. That gave her guardrails—and permission—to keep it simple.

She started sharing one post a week:

- A short reaction to an industry article.
- A reflection on something she was learning.
- A quick takeaway from class discussions.

After four weeks, her engagement increased by four times, she started receiving more connection requests, and she was eventually invited to speak on a panel about her field.

Key Takeaway

She didn't become a full-time content creator. She just became *intentional* about what she shared and how she showed up.

Mini Case Study: Ava—From Invisible to Recognized

Ava ran a small architecture firm. She believed LinkedIn was "only for job seekers." But once she defined her five content pillars—design thinking, sustainable building, mentoring young architects, Texas-based projects, and the business of architecture—she started posting once a week.

A year later, a major developer reached out because they'd been quietly following her posts.

Key Takeaway

Content pillars don't just give you something to post. They make you findable.

Building Your Content Framework

Control Your Narrative by Choosing What You Want to Be Known For

As I just shared, not knowing what to post is one of the most common things I hear from professionals, no matter their experience level. They recognize the need to be more visible online but feel stuck. They either don't want to sound self-serving, or they're worried they'll come across as boring or generic.

But here's the truth: You already have plenty to share.

You just need a simple, repeatable structure that works for *you*.

Let's build that.

This is not about creating more work. It is about giving structure to your voice.

What Is a Content Framework?

Your content framework is made up of content pillars, the core topics you consistently create or engage around.

These pillars will help you do the following:

- Stay consistent in your messaging.
- Build visibility with the right audiences.
- Highlight your expertise in the areas that matter.
- Make your professional reputation easier to validate.

This chapter is about curating those pillars and balancing the professional with the personal, so your profile feels human and not robotic or AI driven.

Reputation Roadmap vs. Random Posting

- Roadmap = strategic, repeatable, reputation-building.
- Random = reactive, inconsistent, forgettable.

Knox POV: "This is where you start controlling the narrative—not by being louder, but by being clearer."

Strategic Effects Lens: Why Pillars Work

- *Observe:* Notice which topics align with your expertise and interests.
- *Orient:* Map those topics into four to six professional pillars and one to two personal ones.
- *Analyze:* Identify which pillars your audience engages with most.
- *Act:* Post, comment, and share intentionally.
- *Repeat:* Remember that consistency compounds trust.

Mini Case Study: William—From Random to Recognizable

William was a VP of sales in tech. His posts were sporadic and unfocused. Together, we built a content framework around four themes: leadership, customer stories, product education, and market trends.

He posted just twice a month, nothing crazy. Within four months, inbound messages from qualified leads started showing up in his inbox.

Key Takeaway

Seniority cannot replace clarity. Clarity creates visibility.

The Four Steps to Using Your Content Pillars

Content pillars are the engine behind a strong digital presence, but don't let that intimidate you. Think of them as training wheels for your content strategy. You don't have to do it all on day one. That is, you can build over time. Additionally, most of this content will be curated when you start. Remember: First, you crawl. Then, you walk. Eventually, you run.

Your pillars give you focus. They help you decide what's worth sharing, and they ensure your audience sees you as consistent, credible, and human. In practice, most professionals do best with the following:

- *Four to six professional topics* where you bring expertise or want to grow into professionally.
- *One to two personal interests* that make you relatable without oversharing.
- *One charitable or cause-related area* that shows your values.

That balance keeps you professional, but also approachable—human, not robotic or AI-like.

Here are the four steps:

1. Identify Key Themes

Choose four to six professional areas that matter most to you. These should connect to your career story: your skills, roles, certifications, or industry trends. This isn't about everything you *could* talk about; it's about what you want to be known for. You will see in my example below, it can be aspirational. The one to two personal interests help people relate and connect with you. And the charitable area also helps humanize you.

2. Create Diverse Content

Start small: one format you're comfortable with. Over time, you can branch out and turn insights into blog posts, quick tips, polls, videos, or curated articles. The pillar stays the same, and the format shifts as you move through *crawl - walk - run.*

3. Maintain Consistency

You do not have to post every day. You don't have to weigh in on every topic. When you do show up, stay consistent. Use your voice. Share your perspective. Over time, this builds recognition and trust.

4. Target Specific Audiences

Each pillar speaks to part of your network. A leadership pillar might connect with executives. A marketing-trends pillar might attract peers. A community-service pillar might spark conversations outside your industry. The point is relevance, not randomness.

Crawl – Walk – Run: How Visibility Actually Grows

Building your digital presence doesn't happen overnight. It is an investment. Think of it like learning a new skill. You don't start by running a marathon; you start by putting on your shoes and maybe running just one mile.

Crawl: Keep It Simple

- Pick three to four content pillars.
- Post or comment once a week, even a single sentence on why you're sharing someone else's article.
- Share relevant links, short reflections, or lessons learned.
- Your only job here is to build the habit of showing up.

Example:

Maya, a product manager, started by commenting twice a week on product marketing posts. No original content. After three months, she was regularly appearing in her network's feed, and recruiters started reaching out.

Walk: Find Your Rhythm

- Create short, repeatable content formats tied to your pillars (e.g., weekly reflections, quick tips, personal POVs).
- Start scheduling posts to build consistency. LinkedIn has a built-in tool to do this for you. It's at the bottom of every post you create.
- Engage more intentionally with others in your niche.

Example:

Raj, a consultant, started a weekly "Tuesday's Take" post where he shared one insight on organizational change. The format became recognizable, and his engagement doubled in six weeks.

Run: Amplify and Experiment

- Layer in videos, carousels, or longer thought leadership posts.
- Show up multiple times a week but strategically, not chaotically.
- Use your content to spark conversations, build authority, and collaborate.

Mini Case Study

Sophia, a marketing strategist, used her content pillars to map out a 90-day posting rhythm. Within three months, she had two new inbound leads, all without "going viral."

Knox POV: "Your goal isn't to be everywhere. Your goal is to build trust through steady, intentional steps. Crawl first. Walk next. Then run."

Pro Tip: You can stay in walk mode forever and still see major results. Most professionals never need to run to build visibility.

Example: Knox's Content Pillars

When I build my own framework, here's how it breaks down:

Professional (four to six):

- Process Reengineering
- Organizational Change Management
- Go-to-Market Strategies
- Digital Marketing Alignment & Messaging
- Learning & Development

Personal (one to two):

- Tacos (yes, they really do connect people!)
- Books I'm Reading (invites conversations and positions me as a thought leader)

Charitable (one):

- She Supply (a nonprofit supporting women's dignity through access to feminine hygiene products) … www.shesupply.org for more information.

Notice what happens here:

- The professional pillars define what I want to be known for and where I add value.
- The personal pillars make me approachable and memorable, without oversharing.

- The charitable pillar shows I care about something beyond my own business.

Together, they humanize me while keeping my content purposeful.

Knox POV: "Your pillars should feel natural to talk about. If you're forcing a topic, it's probably not your pillar."

Mini Case Study: Aspirational Content Pillars

Your content pillars can be aspirational! What do I mean by this?

Take Ryan for example, Ryan earned an engineering degree as an undergrad and has just completed his Master's degree in International Finance. He is interviewing for positions in equity research, so a portion of his content pillars focus on content specific to the job he *wants.*

Aspirational vs. Experienced Pillars

- *Experienced:* what he's already built credibility around.
- *Aspirational:* where he's growing and wants to gain more visibility.

Make It Human

Having only professional content is limiting and, quite frankly, boring. People connect with people.

So, add one to two personal pillars that are light, interesting, and you.

These should never overshadow your expertise, but they should complement it. Think about these:

- Your hobby (ex: photography, running, travel).
- Your background (ex: native Texan, first-gen college grad).
- A random detail that makes you memorable (ex: taco enthusiast).

Sometimes, it's the random things that stick. (Trust me: Tacos have generated more consulting leads for me than SEO ever did.)

Case Study: Make It Human

Some personal topics can be quite benign. Take my friend Ted Rubin and his love for flamboyant socks. This topic stuck with his audiences so well that he has a hashtag for it: #TedSockie. Google it! (Examples are in the QR Code section as well.)

Ted had long enjoyed wearing vibrant, expressive socks, and he'd occasionally wear them knowingly to speaking engagements, letting people glimpse them. After one event, a blogger took a photo of Ted's socks and shared it. Within hours, the online conversation about his socks was everywhere: People asked where he got them, shared their own pairs, and posted images of sock combos.

Suddenly, those socks were a touchpoint, a conversation starter.

That experiment evolved into the #TedSockie tradition. The quirky detail that seemed so personal became an integral part of his brand. People expect it. They ask about it. It makes him memorable.

Ted argues that in a world of polished, professional profiles, it's often the small, human touches that make the biggest difference. Showing an authentic side, even via something as simple as creative socks, turns your digital presence from sterile to real.

Ted on posting about his socks:

"When I returned to Twitter, my feed was jumping. People loved the socks … They asked where I found mine … The next day rolled around, and my socks were still a hot topic."

Ted goes on to say, *"Show people what you do best and enjoy most, and they will enjoy it with you."*

My own love for tacos and my related posts underscores this philosophy.

Knox POV: "In a world full of carefully scrubbed corporate tweets and posts, simply showing your creative, human side has serious value."

Why This Works (and Why You Should Care)

- It **breaks the mold**: In a sea of clean headshots and AI-generated corporate blurbs, a sock photo is unexpected.
- It **invites connection**: People ask about it. They respond. Even if they don't love socks, they can relate to passion and humor.
- It **supports consistency**: Over time, the socks become part of the identity, reinforcing authenticity.
- It **signals confidence**: It shows that you don't have to be perfect; you can be playful and human.

Know Your Audience

A friend's daughter had just finished medical school and was interviewing for a residency program. One of her hobbies was skeet shooting, but it wasn't on her resume or LinkedIn profile.

Her father encouraged her to add it. She resisted. "*That has nothing to do with medicine*," she said.

His response was simple: "*Know your audience. You're applying in Texas. That detail could connect you with the people across the table.*"

Reluctantly, she added it.

Ten minutes into her interview, the conversation turned to skeet shooting. When she spoke with passion about her hobby, the program directors lit up. They were avid shooters themselves and were intrigued that she was involved in a traditionally male-dominated sport. The discussion flowed, and most of the interview centered on that shared interest.

She later told her father: *"That was genius. They offered me the residency, and I know part of it was because they felt a real connection with me."*

Lesson: Know Your Audience

The right personal detail, placed in the right context, can transform an interview, profile, or conversation from transactional to relational.

Three Ways to Apply This Tactic:

1. *Context Matters.* Skeet shooting in Texas? Connection. Skeet shooting on an East Coast application? Maybe not. Every audience has its own cultural ins and outs, so use your hobbies wisely.
2. *Humanize Yourself.* A hobby, cause, or interest can break the ice and shift the tone. It's not about being impressive; it's about being relatable.
3. *Be Intentional.* Don't list everything you've ever done. Choose the detail that fits your audience and supports the impression you want to leave.

Exercise: Build Your Content Framework

Now it's your turn. Pull out your previous exercises or start fresh. Use this format to finalize your content framework:

Professional Pillars (Pick Four to Six)

Start with a big brainstorm. Then narrow it down to the ones you want to *own.* Keep in mind that you do not have to limit what you've done. For example, my MBA students are often in career transitions, moving from one domain of expertise to another. That's okay. Step into it.

I tell them to talk about the things they are interested in and to use their past as a baseline.

Let's take me as an example. I wasn't always a management consultant. My first corporate job was with a small company where my primary focus was sales and operations, but I also had a role in learning and development.

After grad school, I landed a product manager role for a high-tech company. From there I went to quality assurance and process reengineering programs in global manufacturing before turning to organizational change management in the consulting space.

From there it's been running my own boutique consultancy, turned author and public speaker.

Each phase or stage of my career required me to build a bridge from what I was doing to what I wanted to do next. I don't speak or share content on everything I've done in my past. If I did, it would not serve my current or future roles. I prioritize my topics and tweak them from time to time based on my next endeavor.

Knox Note: "You don't have to get it perfect the first time. Pillars evolve with you."

My Professional Pillars (and Why)

These are the pillars I build my content around—because they reflect not just what I do, but how I think, how I solve problems, and how I help people and organizations show up with more clarity and confidence.

1. Process Reengineering

I started my career breaking down systems and rebuilding them for efficiency, clarity, and scale. That discipline has followed me through every role since. Today, I use those same skills in corporate workshops and advisory engagements, helping teams rethink how they work, simplify what's complex, and operate with more intention and less waste.

2. Organizational Change Management (OCM)

Change has been a constant throughout my career, and guiding people through it became a core strength. My OCM background helps leaders do more than implement strategies; it helps them bring their people along. This shows up in everything from my consulting to my speaking engagements, where I teach organizations how to align messaging, empower employees, and create adoption that lasts.

3. Go-to-Market (GTM) Strategies

I've spent years helping products, services, and teams find their path to market. That perspective now fuels my advisory work with start-ups, founders, and product teams. It also anchors my Digital Validation™ program, where I show professionals how to create their own GTM strategy—positioning themselves clearly so opportunities can find them.

4. Digital Marketing Alignment and Messaging

Too many organizations treat digital marketing as a checklist. My focus is on alignment—ensuring content, positioning, and channels reinforce each other. This pillar is central to Digital Validation™: teaching professionals how to shape their online narrative, build trust, and show up consistently in ways that support real business outcomes.

5. Learning and Development (L&D)

Teaching has been a through-line in my career from the beginning. What started in corporate training rooms eventually evolved into my work as an adjunct professor, workshop leader, and course creator. Today, L&D is one of the ways I help professionals level up—whether I'm guiding MBA students, training sales teams, or helping organizations build capability through Digital Validation™. It's the foundation of how I turn complex ideas into practical, actionable learning.

6. Author and Speaker

Writing *Validated* and moving deeper into thought leadership has sharpened the way I teach, communicate, and deliver value. At the same time, my speaking work has grown from workshops to keynote-level sessions where I challenge audiences to rethink visibility, alignment, and digital presence. This pillar reflects the evolution of my career—turning expertise into ideas and ideas into platforms that help people learn, grow, and take action.

Why this matters for the exercise:

You don't just pick topics that sound impressive. You pick the ones that do the following:

- Connect to your current offerings.
- Showcase your expertise.
- Bridge where you've been to where you're going.

Your content pillars should help tell your story!

Back to Pillars: Personal Pillars (Pick One or Two)

Choose topics that are approachable, not too personal, and consistent with the persona you're building and sharing.

Example:

1. Amateur photographer
2. Taco lover

Charity / Social Good (Optional: Pick One or Two)

If you support or volunteer with an organization, this can highlight your values and add dimension to your brand.

Example:

1. Board member, literacy council
2. Habitat for humanity volunteer

Write a one-paragraph persona that ties it all together.

This summary helps guide your voice and messaging. It's your content compass.

Example Persona (Knox):

I'm a management consultant turned author and speaker who thrives on helping organizations rethink how they work. My focus is on process reengineering, organizational change management, go-to-market strategies, and digital marketing alignment, areas where I've built expertise across corporate roles, consulting, and teaching. At the same time, I bring a human side to my presence: sharing my love of tacos, the books I'm reading, and shining a light on charitable organizations like She Supply. My voice is professional but approachable, blending strategy with storytelling, always with the goal of adding value, building trust, and making meaningful connections.

Outside Perspective

"You don't have a business life and a personal life. You're one and the same person. Integrity and reputation used to be two different words. Integrity was what you stood for behind closed doors; reputation was what the public perceived. Now they're the same thing because of full transparency."

—Erik Qualman, SXSW 2025

Qualman has spent more than a decade writing and speaking about how transparency has collapsed the wall between personal and professional identity.

The key takeaway is this: in a transparent world, your content is your reputation.

Statistics

- Only 1 percent of LinkedIn users create original content.
- People who share content receive eight times more profile views.
- 79 percent of people prefer engaging with people who show both expertise and personality.
- Personal stories receive up to five times more engagement.

Strategic Effects and Content Pillars (Act Phase):

- *Observe:* Identify what matters to you and your audience.
- *Orient:* Choose your pillars.
- *Analyze:* See what works.
- *Act:* Post with intention.
- *Repeat:* Refine your pillars over time.

Wrap-Up: Be Intentional About What You Post

Your content framework or content pillars is your blueprint for what you will talk about, how you show up, and how people will remember you.

Don't post randomly. Don't engage aimlessly. Show up with purpose and intention!

Key Takeaways

- You now have content pillars to guide your voice and positioning.
- Content ultimately needs to be human to human focused, not B2B or B2C.
- Do no post randomly. Show up with intention.

QR Code

CHAPTER 11
How to Share Good Stuff: Content Repository & More

Your professional brand is built on trust, and trust is built through adding value consistently over time. In this chapter, I will show you how to plan ahead, stay organized, and source great content that resonates with your audience. The goal is to help you move from "What should I post today?" to "I've got a system that works."

Let's be honest, staring at a blank content window is intimidating.

Most people don't struggle with *whether* to show up online. They struggle with *what* to share.

The good news? One—you now have a solid content framework in place from Chapter 10. Two—you are not required to create every post from scratch. Instead, you will curate content that resonates with you and adds your point of view.

To do this, you will save content in a repository. Later you can batch it and distribute it through a content calendar. It's a simple pipeline: Save → Plan → Publish.

Doing this with consistency, discipline, and intention will help expand your professional digital footprint, increase your visibility, and position you as a subject matter expert or thought leader!

Outside Perspective

In his book, *Getting Things Done*, David Allen says:

"Your mind is for having ideas, not holding them."

A content repository is your external brain. Instead of relying on inspiration to strike at 7 a.m. hopefully before your first meeting of the day, a content repository gives you a system for capturing and storing ideas the moment they happen.

Whether it's a story, article, or spark from a conversation, the goal isn't to use it immediately; it's to make sure it doesn't get lost.

Key Takeaway

Your best content ideas rarely show up when it's convenient. A good system makes sure they don't disappear.

Strategic Effects

Posting without a plan is like throwing darts in the dark. You might hit something now and then, but you won't build momentum or trust. That's where Strategic Effects comes in.

First, *observe*. Watch what actually lands and connects: the posts people comment on, the articles that get shared, and the conversations showing up in your feed or newsletters. These are your signals.

Next, *orient*. Map those signals back to your content pillars: the topics that define your expertise and the story you want to tell online.

, *analyze*. Spot the patterns. What draws engagement? What falls flat? Use those insights to build your repository and your content calendar, so you're not starting from zero every time.

Now, *act*. Schedule your posts, share your POV, and show up with consistency. This is where visibility compounds.

Finally, *repeat*. Review what worked and what didn't, and then refine. Keep the flywheel turning.

This rhythm—observe, orient, analyze, act, and repeat—turns a posting habit into a visibility strategy.

Your content calendar is where that strategy becomes real.

Why It Matters

Most people don't *invest* in the time they spend time online. Instead, they waste it.

The average TikTok session runs about 55 minutes, while the average LinkedIn session barely hits eight minutes. That's not a lack of time. That's a lack of strategy.

People don't struggle to show up. They struggle to invest their time where it pays off and to know *how* to show up with intention and value. A content calendar helps change that.

When you have a plan, your digital presence isn't left to chance. Each post builds on the last, turning casual visibility into sustained credibility. Over time, that consistency compounds trust, and trust is the currency of your professional brand.

And the data backs it up: LinkedIn users who post weekly get five times more profile views than those who don't. Pair that with thoughtful engagement, and your professional reputation compounds faster than any doomscrolling session ever could.

A content calendar gives your strategy structure. A repository gives it fuel. Together, they turn "I should post more" into "I know exactly what's next."

Mini Case Study: Jennifer—Starting Small

Jennifer, a consultant launching a new side business, used to get stuck staring at a blank LinkedIn post box. Together we built a bare-bones repository, a spreadsheet with a handful of articles, and personal story prompts.

She committed to posting just twice a month. Within three months, she wasn't scrambling anymore. She had a vault of at least 40 ideas and a posting rhythm she could trust.

Key Takeaway

Your first system doesn't need to be fancy. It just needs to exist.

Outside Perspectives

"Influence isn't popularity. Influence is trust over time."

—Amanda Russell, author of *The Influencer Code*

"The personal brand that wins isn't the loudest; it's the one that shows up with purpose and generosity."

—Mark Schaefer, author of *Known*

True influence isn't built overnight; it's earned. Mark reminds us to show up with intention; Amanda reminds us why it matters. Consistency builds visibility, but trust turns that visibility into opportunity.

That is the real power of establishing a system. It's not posting more, but earning credibility one interaction at a time.

The Concept of "Shareworthy"

"If you're creating anything, and it's not something that you personally feel good enough to share with your team or your own social circle, then it's not good enough to put into the world."

—John Starkweather, Brand Innovators Interview

When John talks about content being "shareworthy," he's describing more than just quality. He's setting the bar for trust and value.

If you wouldn't proudly share it yourself, why would anyone else?

This idea applies directly to your content repository. Don't fill your vault with fluff. Fill it with content that's worth disrupting someone's scroll. Content that gives them reason to pause and think *that's interesting* or *that's useful information.*

Ask yourself these questions:

- Would I share this with my team or a peer?
- Would this spark curiosity, conversation, or trust?
- Does it align with my professional pillars and add value?

If the answer is no, it doesn't belong in the calendar.

Shareworthy content isn't about perfection. It's about relevance, resonance, and respect for your audience's time.

Core Concepts Covered Previously

The Power of Sharing

- Posts that add value reinforce your credibility, and with consistency over time, build trust.
- Content does not need to be original. Smart professionals curate and aggregate content, and then personalize it with their point of view.

Knox POV:

"You don't need to create everything from scratch, but you do need to make it your own"

You Don't Need to Post Every Day

But you *do* need a plan. Your content calendar is your plan.

When you add a content category to your calendar, tie it back to your professional pillars and the eight purposes of content we covered earlier. That way, every post supports your larger professional brand strategy.

Refresher on the eight purposes of content:

1. Inform / Educate
2. Motivate / Inspire
3. Humanize / Connect
4. Position / Lead
5. Recognize / Reward
6. Entertain / Delight
7. Engage / Converse
8. Promote / Brag

The Three Tools

In Chapter 10 we built out your content pillars: the things that you will focus on posting and commenting about. So now, we no longer need to worry about *what* to post.

Your content repository, content calendar, and editorial calendar will be your tools for staying organized and being consistent in posting on LinkedIn.

Step One: Build Your Content Repository

A content repository is your personal library of ideas, resources, and inspiration, the raw material you'll draw from to build your posts. It's where intentional visibility begins. Instead of relying on last-minute inspiration, you collect content that aligns with your professional pillars, tag it for easy retrieval, and keep it ready to fuel your content calendar.

Staying organized with post or content ideas and your go-to sources for content to share are part of a system that will help you maintain consistency. Think of a content repository as your idea vault.

It's where you collect anything that sparks a thought, teaches something, or aligns with your content pillars. Think of it as your personal library of shareable material, the *fuel* for your content calendar.

Your repository might include the following:

- Articles from trusted sources (*McKinsey Quarterly*, *Harvard Business Review*, trade publications, blogs, etc.).
- Thoughtful LinkedIn posts or quotes from leaders in your space.
- Podcast episodes, videos, or talks worth sharing.
- Photos, graphics, infographics, or screenshots.
- Notes, bullet points, and half-baked ideas you'll shape later.

Why It Matters

You can't schedule what you don't have.

A calendar is only as strong as the content behind it. If your vault is empty, you're back to scrambling. If it's full, you're never starting from zero. You already have a steady stream of shareable material ready to go.

The key isn't to make it fancy. It's to make it easy. Start with a simple Excel or Google sheet. Create the following columns:

- Source—where it came from (e.g., LinkedIn post or podcast episode).
- Link or File—so you can find it fast later.
- Theme or Topic—what the content is about.
- Content Pillar—which of your pillars it supports.
- POV Idea—a quick note on *your* take or why it matters.

This step alone eliminates the "blank screen panic" many people face when they want to post but don't know where to start. When it's time to plan your content, you'll already have a vault of material ready to go.

Pro Tip: Do not overthink organization in the beginning. A messy but active repository beats a perfect system that doesn't get used. You can always upgrade tools later once your volume grows.

Your repository is where intention starts.

Once your vault is full, the next step is putting it to work. That's where your content calendar comes in. Your calendar is where it comes to life.

Real-Life Repository Entry

Source: Alexandra Camp (LinkedIn)

Content: "What role does empathy play at work?" (More than you think.)

My POV: Empathy isn't just HR fluff; it's a leadership lever. When you lead with empathy, you shift from managing tasks to nurturing trust and performance. For my audience of rising professionals, that means: ask good questions, listen more than you talk, and then share what you heard. The best leaders are focused on relationships not transactions.

This idea, source, and notes is a valuable post just waiting to be fully written and scheduled by you.

Content Pillar: Leadership / Professional Growth

Why It Matters

This post gives a modern angle on leadership relevance.

This example repository entry becomes a launchpad for a unique story and conversation starting post.

Mini Case Study: Arun—Building a Content Infrastructure

Arun, a VP of marketing, wanted his team to show up consistently on LinkedIn. Instead of pushing them to "be creative," he built a shared repository and calendar system with weekly themes tied to their content pillars.

In six months, their collective engagement grew four times, and a lead generating pipeline started coming through via LinkedIn messaging.

Key Takeaway

Motivation fades. Systems scale.

Exercise: Fill Your Content Repository

1. Set a timer for 15 minutes.
2. Find and save five pieces of content that align with your professional pillars: an article, a quote, a podcast, a post, or a statistic.
3. Drop each one into your repository with at least one line of your POV or why it matters to you or your audience.

That's it. You've just taken the hardest step: starting.

A repository gives you raw material, but a calendar turns that material into momentum.

Step Two: Build Your Content Calendar

A content calendar is your posting plan, the engine that turns ideas into action. It organizes what you'll share, when you'll share it, and where it will go. Instead of scrambling to post in the moment, you work from a roadmap that keeps your messaging intentional and consistent.

A content calendar isn't about making your life complicated. It's about making it easier.

Think of it as your playbook: Instead of scrambling every Monday asking, "What do I post this week?" you already know what's coming. That clarity frees you up to focus on bigger things.

When I started, I was in the *crawl* stage. My calendar lived in an Excel spreadsheet with just the basics. Later, when I moved into the *walk* stage, I leveraged a shared Google sheet and then Trello for easier collaboration with my team. For larger clients in the *run* stage, we've used enterprise tools like Sprinklr, Sprout Social, and Hootsuite. (I'm not advocating for any one tool here, just showing that as your needs grow, so will your system.)

For our purposes, let's keep it simple and start with Excel. I'll share a visual example in the QR Code section.

Here are the essentials to include in your content calendar:

- *Date*—when you'll publish or schedule the post.
- *Copy*—the words you'll use.
- *Images*—the photo, graphic, or visual to pair with the post.
- *Link*—any URL you're sharing (LinkedIn usually pulls in a preview image).
- *Content Category*—which content pillar your post supports.
- *Hashtag*—one or two hashtags (#) are ways to index your content, making it easer to find.

If you're working with a team, you can also add these columns:

- *Approval*—a quick checkmark to show it's ready to publish.
- *Status*—draft, ready, scheduled, or published.
- *Platform*—useful if you're posting in more than one place.

Once you've got this set up, the magic happens: batching content. Instead of creating one post at a time, you can knock out a month (or more) in one sitting.

I like to joke that I grew up a Dallas Cowboys fan when they were good. It's been 29 years and counting since then, so now, if I sit down to watch a game, I'll usually have my laptop open. While the Cowboys struggle with consistency, I'm winning in batching content to make sure my game plan is solid.

Knox POV:

"Consistency beats scrambling every time."

And when you want your content to do more than just show up—when you want it to *lead somewhere*—that's where your editorial calendar becomes your map.

Mini Case Study—Crawl to Walk

When I first launched my Digital Validation™ course, I kept my content calendar simple: just an Excel sheet that I updated every Sunday night. I batched my posts for the week, scheduled them, and stopped relying on "inspiration" to strike.

After three months of consistent posting, my course views jumped 40 percent, and inbound leads doubled.

As things grew, I shifted from Excel to Trello. Moving from Excel to Trello didn't make my process more complicated; it made it faster. It allowed for smoother collaboration with my content assistant, easier batching, and a clear snapshot of what was coming next.

That's the whole point of moving from *crawl to walk*: your system evolves as your visibility grows. When your ideas have a home and a plan, posting stops being a guessing game and becomes a rhythm.

Step Three: Build Your Editorial Calendar

An editorial calendar is your strategy map. It outlines the big picture of what topics you'll talk about, when you'll highlight them, and who you want to engage with.

While a content calendar focuses on what to post and when, an editorial calendar connects those posts to a larger story, ensuring your visibility has direction, not just activity.

If your content calendar is the engine and your repository is the fuel, your editorial calendar is the map.

An editorial calendar is a strategic planning tool that outlines what topics you will talk about, when you'll talk about them, and who you want to engage with over time.

Unlike a content calendar, which focuses on scheduling posts, an editorial calendar gives your content direction and purpose. It connects your themes, audiences, and timing into a clear narrative arc.

An editorial calendar is the strategy layer that answers: *What are you talking about, and who are you talking to?*

This isn't about posting more. It's about posting with intention. An editorial calendar helps you plan the following:

- The themes you want to focus on each month (aligned with your content pillars).
- The key audiences you want to reach (e.g., specific people, industries, or groups).
- The timing of campaigns or personal milestones (e.g., upcoming talks, product launches, conference season, promotion cycles).

A content calendar tells you *when* to post. An editorial calendar tells you *why* you're posting and *who* it's for.

Mini Case Study: Chad Costas—Planning, Pivoting, and Course Correction

When Chad Costas and I sat down to map out his visibility strategy, the breakthrough didn't come from some complicated framework. It came from a simple question: "*What would happen if you treated your own visibility like a product launch, with a plan, test, and refinement cycle?*"

That clicked for him immediately.

Chad comes from a world where execution matters but adaptability matters even more. As he put it during our conversation: "*Everyone needs a plan ... but everyone also gets punched in the face. That's why you course-correct.*"

So we built him a personal editorial calendar—not as a rigid posting schedule but as a navigation tool. Like sailing, he said: You point the boat in the right direction, but you tack as the wind shifts.

Within weeks these were his results:

- His engagement sharpened.
- His content became more intentional.
- Senior leadership started noticing him more.
- His visibility at work changed.

Key Takeaway

A calendar isn't about *control*. It's about direction and correction—a simple system that helps you adjust course without losing momentum.

Pro Tip: Start small. Pick two or three themes for the quarter and five to 10 people or groups with whom you want to build visibility. Layer those onto your content calendar, so your posts and engagement work together.

Statistics

- LinkedIn reports that users who post weekly see five times more profile views than those who don't.
- Regular posts can increase engagement by up to 11 times.
- The brain processes visual content 60,000 times faster than text. And people retain 80 percent of what they see, compared to 20 percent of what they read. So be sure to include visual content with your posts!
- LinkedIn posts with images get two times more comments than those without images.
- B2B buyers consume an average of eight pieces of content before engaging with a brand.
- People remember stories 22 times more than facts alone.
    - Facts tell. Stories sell.

TOOL	FUNCTION	METAPHOR	KEY QUESTION ANSWERED
Content Repository	Collect and organize ideas	Fuel	"What could I share?"
Content Calendar	Plan and schedule posts	Engine	"What will I share and when?"
Editorial Calendar	Align themes, audience, and timing	Map	"Why am I sharing this—and with whom?"

Quick Reference Guide

Strategic Effects Lens: Why Systems Work

- *Observe:* Notice what consistently captures your attention—and why.
- *Orient:* Organize it into a repository with clear pillars.
- *Analyze:* Spot which themes resonate most with your audience.
- *Act:* Schedule intentionally. Show up with purpose.
- *Repeat:* Consistency compounds.

How Often Should I Post?

I get asked this question all the time. My answer? *It depends.*

What stage are you in? (Crawl? Walk? Run?) Are you posting just to post, or is there a reason to post? Are you running a campaign?

I recognize that we are all starting at different places in our careers and in building our professional brand. If you're new, then one or two times per month is fantastic! And when you get comfortable with that, you can ramp it up.

If you are already comfortable in posting, then aim for four to five times per month. And if you're already doing this, then aim for two posts per week.

Do Not Forget About Commenting

You've heard me say this throughout the book: Join the conversation. Social media is not *social* if people are not commenting or engaging. Around 80 percent of your visibility comes from commenting on other people's posts.

So share! Share an experience. Share a point of view.

Ask questions. Start a conversation. Be interested.

Be open to learning and growing!

Knox POV: The goal isn't perfection. It's consistency and value. Share content that's good, not perfect. Batch your content, build your system, and keep showing up.

Key Takeaways

- Content calendars and content repositories are designed to make your life easier, so you have a process for finding things to post and a process for getting them posted.
- Repository = fuel. Your content repository is where intentional visibility starts. Collect, tag, and save what's worth sharing, so you're never starting from zero.
- Calendar = engine. A content calendar turns scattered ideas into a consistent system. Plan it once, and show up many times.
- Quality over quantity. Use John Starkweather's "Shareworthy" test: Would you share it yourself? If not, it doesn't belong on your calendar.
- Trust > Popularity. As Amanda Russell says, "Influence isn't popularity. Influence is trust over time." Consistency compounds credibility.
- Engagement multiplies reach. Some 80 percent of your LinkedIn visibility comes from commenting and conversation—not just posting.

QR Code

CHAPTER 12
The Three Rules of Social Media: Engage, Engage, Engage

Perhaps you've heard the three rules of real estate: location, location, location. I have adapted those same rules, but applied them to social media.

The three rules of social media are engage, engage, engage!

We get distracted by flash. Influencers. Follower counts. Likes.

But real traction—the kind that builds trust, opens doors, and creates opportunities—comes from showing up and engaging like a human.

Conversations are king! Conversations build relationships.

Outside Perspective

Ted Rubin, author of *Return on Relationship*, writes:

> *"Relationships are the new currency. Honor them, invest in them, and start measuring your ROR."*

Ted's concept of return on relationship (ROR) aligns perfectly with this chapter. Engagement is not about vanity metrics. Instead it is about building the kind of trust that actually compounds over time.

Key Takeaway

Engagement is not a tactic. It is a trust and relationship strategy.

Statistic #1 for LinkedIn

For me, this is the most powerful statistic about LinkedIn:

- Right now, 80 percent of your LinkedIn visibility is derived from engagement, from publicly joining (or starting) conversations through the comment section of each post.

I also like to tie in this paradox:

If a tree falls in the woods, and no one is there to hear it, does it make a sound?

This can also be applied to your social media post.

If you post something on social media and no one comments on it, will anyone see it?

My answer is no. If no one engages with your post, then it's a dead post, and no one will see it. Or at least, very few.

Algorithms reward engagement heavily (not that I want to talk about algorithms or have you create content that is focused solely on the algorithms; content must add value). LinkedIn posts that generate comments are treated as more valuable and get boosted in reach.

The key point is that social media was designed to be social, not to be another broadcasting platform. Posts with zero engagement are ultimately seen as noise, receiving less time in the newsfeed and becoming that tree that falls in the woods.

H2H > B2B or B2C

You've also heard me espouse that it's about human to human (H2H) over business to business (B2B) or business to consumer (B2C).

Here's why: People do business with people. People follow people. People trust people.

Trust doesn't come from shouting at the Internet. (There's that concept again: *broadcasting.*) It comes from consistent, thoughtful interactions, especially on LinkedIn. This is where your presence validates your reputation.

In the early days of social media, marketing was viewed as someone with a megaphone shouting their messages to people.

In many instances, the social media space has started to become that marketing megaphone where people are broadcasting (or shouting) their messages as opposed to creating engaging content or engaging campaigns.

So How Do I Engage More on LinkedIn?

Think of LinkedIn like a dinner party. You walk into a room full of people, some of whom you know and some you don't. Now ask yourself: *What do I do?* Do you hide in the corner, hoping someone will notice you? Do you hover quietly on the sidelines, listening but never joining in? Or do you circulate, introduce yourself, and engage in conversation?

We all know what happens at a real dinner party. If you stay in the corner, no one remembers you were even there. If you dominate the table by talking only about yourself, people tune you out. But if you listen first, add thoughtful comments, and gradually build connections, you leave having formed real relationships.

The same applies to LinkedIn. Too many professionals show up as lurkers: scrolling, consuming, and maybe liking a post here or there but never really participating. And then they wonder why their visibility and influence stay low.

On LinkedIn, engagement is the key. It helps people get to know you. Social media is designed to be social, so use LinkedIn to connect, learn, and share! (People aren't on social media to be sold to. So don't lead with that!)

So before you think about posting more content, start by listening. Pay attention to the conversations happening in your space. Then step in, add your perspective, and contribute something of value. That's how trust gets built online, the same way it does face to face: through consistent, human interaction.

How to Frame Engagement

Think of it this way: Broadcasting is like putting up a billboard on the side of a highway. It might be effective for a moment in letting someone in a car going 65 mph know about nearby services such as gas and food. (I live in Texas, so it'd be a truck and our highway speeds are much faster! Lol)

But true engagement, not broadcasting, is more like a coffee shop in a small town. The tables tend to be communal and everyone tends to chat one another up whether they know them or not. LinkedIn should be viewed more like that small town. While you know people (aka, your contact list), there are other conversations (i.e., posts) taking place, and each one offers the opportunity to join that conversation thread.

When you do this consistently on LinkedIn from a position of adding value and being interested in the person, post, or conversation, then you wind up building relationships and establishing your voice and thought leadership.

Statistics

- On LinkedIn, posts with five or more comments get four times more views on average than those with no comments.
- Engaging with other people's posts doubles your profile visibility because every comment puts you in front of a second audience: the poster's network.

Case Study

Let's take a comment I made on a Gary Vaynerchuk post several years ago. For those who don't know Gary V, he is an entrepreneur, a bestselling author, and one of the most visible people in modern marketing. He is known for his no-nonsense takes on business, brand, and the power of social media.

While I have met and interviewed Gary multiple times at venues like SxSW, Gary doesn't know me from Adam, and we are not first-degree connections on social media. (Hey Gary, if you ever see this, let's change that! Lol. *Hey, you never know!*)

Several years ago, Gary posted something on LinkedIn that deeply resonated with me. I invested a little time (probably not more than 10 minutes) writing a short, reflective comment that shared some of my personal experience.

On my comment, I received 271 likes, 40 comments from others that drove six or more separate conversations and 10 new LinkedIn connections.

Key Takeaway

Conversations (i.e., social media engagement) drive relationships.

Mindset Shift: Spending Time vs. Investing Time

Let's step back for a moment and talk about spending time versus investing time.

We've all been there: thumb scrolling through an endless feed, not even sure what we're looking for. Before smartphones, it was channel surfing, flipping through television stations hoping something better would appear on the next channel.

Today it's TikTok, Instagram Reels, and YouTube Shorts. The platforms are engineered to keep us hooked. The average TikTok session is 55 minutes. For LinkedIn, it's closer to eight minutes.

That gap tells a story. TikTok and Instagram are designed for entertainment, distraction, and instant dopamine hits. LinkedIn, on the other hand, is designed for professional connection.

Here's the difference in where your time goes: When you scroll TikTok or Instagram without intention, you're *spending* time. Like spending money on something you don't really need, time disappears the moment you swipe to the next video. There's no return. No ROI.

Now, what if you redirected just 10 minutes of that time? Ten minutes carved out of your TikTok or Instagram habit and reinvested into LinkedIn.

Not scrolling aimlessly. Instead, you are showing up with purpose. Liking a colleague's post. Adding a thoughtful comment. Jumping into a conversation where your expertise adds value.

That's no longer spending time. That's *investing* time.

And just like investing money, the payoff is compounding. One thoughtful comment may put your name in front of dozens of people you don't know yet. Ten comments a week may draw hundreds of profile views.

Over time, those micro-interactions accumulate into trust, visibility, and opportunities.

Think of it this way: Doomscrolling is like pulling the lever on a slot machine, hoping something fun or shiny pops up. Intentional engagement on LinkedIn is like putting money into a retirement account. One is gone in a flash; the other grows steadily over time.

Social media can either drain you or build you. The deciding factor is not the platform; it's how you use your minutes.

Time spent is gone. Time invested pays you back.

Lurkers watch, leaders engage.

Mini Case Study: From Ghost Mode to Growth Mode

I know two executives. They have similar networks and similar expertise.

One spent his time on LinkedIn in silence: scrolling but never engaging. The other one invested just 10 minutes a day liking, commenting, and jumping into conversations that mattered to her.

Six months later, their results could not have been more different. The lurker's profile was static, invisible, and forgotten. But the engager? She had dozens of new connections, a handful of inbound opportunities, and a growing reputation in their similar space.

She added value, built trust, and became seen.

Key Takeaway

Visibility compounds through engagement. Lurkers watch conversations, while leaders join them.

Strategic Effects

The difference between passively scrolling and intentionally engaging isn't just about how you use your time; it's about the ripple effect that it creates.

When you scroll without purpose, you're observing but not participating.

No impact. No signal. No proof of presence.

When you intentionally show up and engage even for just a few minutes, you shift from passive observer to active participant. And that is how you start to build visibility.

This is classic Strategic Effects in action: Small actions compound over time. Add value. Build trust. Be seen, and create opportunity.

A single thoughtful comment can put you in front of hundreds of people you've never met. Ten comments a week can expand your reach and reputation exponentially.

I'm not the only one saying this. Some of the sharpest voices in marketing have been pointing to this exact dynamic for years: Engagement is where the real ROI lives.

Updated Strategic Effects

Through a Strategic Effects lens, here's how engagement compounds:

Observe: Notice what sparks real conversation. Pay attention to posts that make you pause, think, or type a response—those moments show you where your voice naturally fits and where you can add value.

Orient: Get intentional about *who* you want to show up for. Identify 10–20 people or companies whose conversations you want to be part of: industry voices, potential partners, executives, colleagues, or people you genuinely admire. This is your digital neighborhood. (I have an Excel spreadsheet with my list. It helps remind me to check in on people, companies, and topics that I want to be a part of.)

Analyze: Look at what happens when you engage. Which comments get replies? Which ones attract profile views? Which threads lead to DMs or deeper conversations? This tells you where your presence is actually landing.

Act: Show up daily (or as consistently as your life allows) with purpose:

comment early, comment thoughtfully, and add insight rather than noise. Don't wait for the perfect post. Jump into the conversations that matter to you.

Repeat: Every meaningful comment is a small deposit into the trust bank. Over time, those deposits compound, and your name starts showing up in all the right places. This is how you become familiar, credible, and top-of-mind—long before anyone reads your resume or visits your website.

Outside Perspective

Ted Rubin says it wonderfully. (If you don't know Ted, he's the author of *Return on Relationship*, and it's a must read!). In a LinkedIn post, Ted says:

> *"Social isn't a billboard; it's a living, breathing conversation. Too many small businesses forget that posting is only the start. The real ROI comes when you engage, respond, and build trust through interaction."*

He goes on, drawing from his book:

> *"... every reply, every 'thank you,' every moment you make a customer feel seen is compounding value. Ignore it, and you're literally leaving money, loyalty, and opportunity on the table."*

Too many people—and too many brands—skip this step entirely. They treat engagement like background noise, when in reality, it's free visibility just waiting to be activated. Someone took time out of their day to talk about you or your work. Ignoring that isn't neutral; it's costly.

And here's what most professionals and companies miss: Silence keeps you invisible.

If you don't show up in the moments when people are already paying attention, you disappear from the conversation.

This isn't a social media tactic problem. It's a mindset problem.

The individuals and brands who win are the ones who answer the knock. They show up in the comments, acknowledge the tag, and turn a small moment into a relationship. That's how trust is built. That's how loyalty forms. And that's how opportunities start.

Visibility is earned in the replies. Show up when it counts.

Knox POV: After consulting thousands of professionals, here's the pattern I've seen over and over again: People think visibility comes from posting, but posting is only half the equation. The real visibility—the kind that leads to opportunities—comes from engaging with others.

When you reply, you become memorable. When you acknowledge someone, you become human. When you show up consistently, you become trusted.

Every comment is a small moment of proof that you're paying attention, that you care, and that you're someone worth following.

Visibility is earned in the replies. That's where reputations are built and careers gain momentum.

Invest Your Time, Don't Just Spend It

We spend time on most social media platforms doom scrolling through mindless content.

I want to encourage you to shift your mindset a little. On LinkedIn, we should be thinking about it as investing time through adding value, nurturing relationships, learning new things, and being present.

Time invested wisely compounds, leading to increased visibility, positioning us as subject matter experts and thought leaders, increasing our relevance, and expanding our digital footprints.

When done correctly, it can build our Digital Validation™, a strong, consistent and professional online presence. After all, our (digital) reputations will precede us.

Crawl – Walk – Run

Okay, what about a framework to do this? Similar to what I shared previously, let's focus on crawl –walk – run.

Start small, and build on your success.

Crawl

Follow. Connect. Like.

Start with the smallest time commitment, allowing you to get more familiar with LinkedIn and helping you discover its value:

- Follow people who share valuable insights.
- Like content that resonates with your values.
- Connect with intention, and when you do, add a personal note. (Seriously, the note makes all the difference.)

Pro Tip: Swap 10 minutes of scrolling on other platforms with 10 minutes on LinkedIn. Like five posts a day. That's it. But do it consistently.

Walk

Comment. Join Conversations. Show Up.

The next level up is where the real magic starts: Comments create visibility.

But not just "Congrats!" or "Love this."

Make your comments mini thought-leadership moments.

There are four powerful types of comments:

1. Experience-Based: Share what worked or didn't work for you.
2. Opinion-Based: Respectfully challenge or expand on the post.
3. Expansive/Building: Add new insight to the discussion.
4. Engaging/Conversational: Ask questions. Be curious.

Remember, 80 percent of your visibility comes from commenting.

Run

Share Your POV and Original Content

This is where trust compounds, but it can take more in terms of a time commitment.

When you consistently create and share content, such as short form, long form, articles, or videos, you tell your story. You shape your reputation. You expand your digital footprint, establish yourself as a subject matter expert, and build your Digital Validation™.

Your content becomes searchable and adds to your professional social proof. When someone Googles you (and they will), they will find your professional-based content!

The 3–2–1 Engagement Rule

To make this practical and not overwhelming, follow this rule to get started. Each week complete the following:

- Three thoughtful comments on posts of people who you admire.
- Two comments on industry-related posts.
- One repost with added POV.

This rhythm builds consistency, visibility, and authority, but the key is consistency!

Mini Case Study

One well-placed comment can change everything. I mentioned the Gary Vaynerchuk post earlier: A single thoughtful comment led to 271 likes, 40 replies, and 10 new connections. Why did it resonate? Because it told a story!

Never underestimate the power of public conversations. Here's the secret: It's not just about showing up; it's about *how* you show up. And one of the best ways to do that is by telling better stories.

Mini Case Study

Priya was a marketing manager who had been on LinkedIn for years without posting or commenting on anything. She was a "lurker." She decided to start by commenting once a day on content from people she admired.

Within 45 days, she saw a measurable uptick in connection requests and profile views. More importantly, she was in conversations she used to only read.

Key Takeaway

Visibility isn't always about posting first. Showing up through comments is often the best way to gain visibility and build trust.

Stories Build Connection

Facts inform. Stories connect. As the saying goes, facts tell, stories sell. A fact might get someone's attention for a moment, but a story is what makes them remember you and want to continue the conversation.

If you want to learn to tell stories better, study comedians. The best comedians aren't just funny; they are world-class storytellers. They take a simple observation, often something you've experienced yourself, and spin it into a short narrative that draws you in, sets the scene, and then lands a punchline. The whole thing might take 30 seconds, but you're hooked.

That's the power of a story well told.

The same applies to engagement on LinkedIn. A thoughtful, story-driven comment, such as, "That reminds me of when …" or "I saw something similar happen in my team …" stands out from the sea of generic "Great post!" replies. It humanizes you. It validates your expertise. It shows that you are intentional and thoughtful in how you engage on the platform. And it invites the original poster and their network to see you as someone worth following.

A Simple Story Framework for Engagement

When you're crafting a short LinkedIn comment or post, think in three beats:

1. Setup—Introduce the situation quickly.
2. Tension/Observation—Share the challenge, conflict, or surprising detail.
3. Punchline/Point—Deliver the insight or takeaway.

That's it. Three steps: short, tight, and engaging.

Example 1: The Generic Comment

- "Great post!"

While this is positive, it is forgettable. It does not add value, invite conversation, or differentiate you.

Do not do this!

Example 2: Same Thought, Story-Driven

- Setup: "This reminds me of when our team rolled out a new CRM a few years ago."
- Tension/Observation: "At first, no one wanted to use it. The feedback was brutal. People said it slowed them down."
- Punchline/Point: "The turning point was when we focused on just one feature that actually made their jobs easier. Adoption took off from there. Totally agree that focusing on the *value* to the user changes everything."

Why is this one better? It's still short, but now you've shared a quick story, validated the original point, and added credibility. That makes you memorable.

Example 3: Micro-Observation (Comedian Style)

- Setup: "Funny how tech rollouts feel like gym memberships."
- Tension/Observation: "Everyone signs up excited, but within weeks most people stop showing up."
- Punchline/Point: "The only way it sticks is if they see results fast; otherwise the enthusiasm disappears. That's why quick wins matter."

This example sticks because it is a metaphor-driven mini-story—short, witty, and aligned with the original topic.

Stories like these humanize you. They show experience, invite connection, and spark replies. When you do this consistently, you're not just part of the conversation; you become someone others look for when they want real insight.

Whether you're on stage, on a podcast, or in a LinkedIn comment thread, this framework pulls people in and leaves them with something they'll remember. When you do this consistently, you stop being just another voice in the feed. You become someone worth engaging with.

Here's what this looks like in practice. Notice how the right story turns a throwaway comment into something memorable.

GENERIC COMMENT	STORY-DRIVEN COMMENT
"Great post!"	"This takes me back to when our team rolled out a new CRM. At first, no one wanted to use it. It slowed everything down. The turning point was focusing on one feature that made their lives easier. Adoption took off from there. Totally agree with your point."
"Love this!"	"I saw something similar when I led a product launch. Everyone was excited on day one, but enthusiasm dipped fast. Quick wins and early feedback loops made all the difference."
"So true."	"Funny how tech rollouts are like gym memberships: lots of sign-ups but few stick around. The key is making it easy to see results early."

Summary: Why Engagement Wins

Let's bring it home:

- Visibility: Comments show you exist.
- Trust: Engagement builds reputation.
- Community: Relationships start with interactions.
- Proof: Public comments beat private thoughts.

Strategic Effects

- *Observe:* Notice who in your network is already shaping conversations.
- *Orient:* Identify where your voice adds value (topic + people).
- *Analyze:* Engagement builds visibility faster than posting in isolation.
- *Act:* Comment, share, and converse with intention.
- *Repeat:* Relationships compound when you show up consistently.

Final Word

You do not need to be the loudest. You do not need to go viral. You just need to be intentional, consistent, and human.

And, of course, you need to follow the three rules of social media: Engage. Engage. Engage.

People who win at social media aren't the ones shouting the loudest. They are the ones showing up intentionally and strategically.

As Amanda Russell reminds us, "Influence is trust over time." Every like, comment, and reply is a brick in that foundation.

Key Takeaways

- Engagement is the engine behind visibility, trust, and opportunity.
- 80 percent of your visibility comes from commenting and participating, not just posting.
- Small, consistent actions compound. It's about showing up intentionally.
- Stories make your engagement memorable and shareworthy.

- You don't need to be loud; you need to be consistent, human, and present.
- Be shareworthy. Be human. Be intentional.

QR Code

CHAPTER 13
Bonus Materials

Where do you put all the leftovers from all the other chapters or the things that really could not make it to the cutting room floor? You put them in a section called Bonus Materials!

But let's also be honest. Not everything fits neatly into a five-module course or a 12 chapter book. Some insights, stories, and frameworks deserve a space of their own. Think of this chapter as the bonus round—the practical tools, expanded ideas, and real stories that deepen what you've already learned.

This chapter reinforces a simple truth: Digital Validation™ is not a one-time event. It's a disciplined, long game of visibility, trust, and proof. Each of these frameworks connects back to the core ideas you've already explored.

Outside Perspective

Peter Drucker, renowned educator of management theory, on execution and preparation:

> *"Plans are only good intentions unless they immediately degenerate into hard work."*

We have spent the last eleven chapters learning the tools and building the plans. Let's put them into action to make the changes we need!

Dinner Party Analogy

We just covered the dinner party metaphor in Chapter 12. But there's another point that I would like to make. It consists of two parts.

Part One: Don't Be That Person

Would you ever walk into a dinner party, stand on a chair, and shout, "Buy this product!" or "Check out my resume!" Of course not. That would be weird and off-putting.

Instead, you would ease into a group of people. You would listen. You would ask thoughtful questions. Eventually, you would find your way into a conversation and share something or add value to it.

Social media should be no different.

Yet we've all had *that* person who, as soon as you connect, tries to sell you something.

My response? Disconnect. And in some cases, block.

Part Two: Social Selling, Revisited

Much like I think the term *personal branding* has been bastardized from its original meaning, the same goes for the term *social selling.*

Originally, social selling was the process of using social networks, most often LinkedIn, to identify, connect with, and build trust-based relationships with potential buyers, rather than jumping straight into a hard pitch.

Social selling has become all about spamming DMs or posting endless sales offers.

Your purpose on LinkedIn should be focused on creating value, demonstrating expertise, and nurturing conversations and relationships. Period.

When someone is ready, *they* initiate the conversations with you because you are the trusted, go-to resource.

Dinner Party Final Points

When your goal is to grow your reputation, increase visibility, and build real relationships, then treat social platforms like that dinner party. Be respectful and helpful. Join the conversations. Get to know others. Thank the host and hostess.

Lastly, focus on the following:

- *Being relationship-driven, not transactional.* The goal is to build credibility and rapport first.
- *Establishing content as social or professional proof.* Share insights, stories, and helpful resources, so prospects see you as relevant and trustworthy.
- *Listening as much as speaking.* Pay attention to your network's posts, pain points, and signals, and then engage thoughtfully.
- *Taking a long-game approach.* A sale might come months or years down the road, but the connection pays dividends through referrals, introductions, and influence.

When you embrace this mindset the magic can happen.

Case Study: When Relationships Become Revenue

As a small business owner and consultant, I can tell you that sometimes you genuinely don't know where the next client will come from. I gave you the Dell example earlier, but here's another one that illustrates how Digital Validation™ works in real life.

Take my friend John. We've known each other since we were kids at a summer camp in the Texas Hill Country. Over the years we kept up loosely, mostly through social media and occasionally on LinkedIn. John works in a niche sales industry with major players like GE, so our worlds didn't really overlap professionally.

Then one day, out of the blue, he called.

He wanted to "talk shop," so we spent almost an hour walking through challenges he was facing at the smaller company he'd just joined. I asked questions, listened, offered perspective, and shared a few actionable ideas.

No pitch. No offer. No "here's my rate card."

Just value. Just conversation. Just what you'd do at a dinner party when someone sits beside you and asks for advice.

He thanked me, and we went on with our lives.

Three months later, he called again—with news. He had pitched my services internally, secured a budget, and wanted to bring me in to help fix the very issues we discussed on that first call.

What I didn't know at the time was this: John had been quietly following my posts, insights, and career updates for years. (Yes, John was a LinkedIn lurker!)

My content built familiarity. My consistency built trust. And that one conversation—the one where I wasn't trying to sell—confirmed that I could help.

This is how Digital Validation™ works in the real world:

- Relationship-first: The connection already existed.
- Content as social proof: He had context for what I do.
- Listening before advising: The conversation added value.
- Long game: The opportunity surfaced organically.

No funnel. No pitch deck. No outreach campaign. Just presence, trust, and being helpful when it counted.

Key Takeaway

Show up consistently, add value when it matters, and people will remember you long after the conversation ends.

Strategic Effects: Observe and Orient

Pay attention to the conversation before you speak. Ask questions. Get to know your audience.

This helps you focus on building relationships, not closing transactions.

Progression of a LinkedIn Strategy

Digital Validation™ does not happen all at once. Instead, it unfolds over time. Here's the roadmap:

- *Profile*: Start by organizing your storefront. Make it easy for people to know who you are.
- *Content*: Establish your voice. Use consistent content pillars to show your expertise. Commenting should be part of your content strategy.
- *Add Value*: Make sure that your content (comments and posts) is helpful.

- *Comment*: Do not limit yourself to posts. Join other people's conversations.
- *Conversation*: As you build relationships on LinkedIn, you can continue them through emails, phone calls, or Zoom calls, and meet in real life. Just continue the dialogue.
- *Relationship*: Real connections lead to real opportunities.

Relationship-building is a long game, but it's the only one that builds trust!

"Five Ways to Connect" Framework

Think of this as a quick gut-check before you show up online. Too often, people overthink their presence or default to pitching, when the real goal is connection.

These five reminders are about how to be human in digital spaces and make your interactions magnetic instead of forgettable.

1. *Be transparent.*

   If you're sharing something from your employer or client, say so. People trust what they can see. Share what you stand for, what you're learning, or even where you've made mistakes. Vulnerability done right is credibility.

2. *Be positive.*

   Negativity repels; positivity attracts. Your outlook sets the tone for how others perceive you. Even when you're tackling tough topics, a constructive angle keeps people engaged.

3. *Be interested.*

   Don't just broadcast; participate. Ask questions. Comment thoughtfully. Signal that you care about others' ideas. Interest builds reciprocity.

4. *Be interesting.*

   Facts tell; stories sell. Add your point of view. Share an experience or perspective that only you could provide. This is where your personality comes through.

5. *Keep it simple.*

   Clarity beats cleverness every time. Online, people skim. If they can't get your point in a quick glance, you've lost them.

Think about this framework as things that make you a great guest at a dinner party. Show up authentically (transparent), bring good energy (positive), listen (interested), share a memorable story (interesting), and don't hog the conversation (simple and clear).

Progression to Trust Ladder (Level of Control)

Most brands still think the way to win is by keeping a tight grip on the message. Ads. Billboards. Polished taglines.

Here's the truth: Control does not equal trust.

- Brand → Customer

  Ads and official messaging are carefully controlled, but people know that they are staged, so they sit at the bottom of the trust ladder.

- Celebrity → Customer

  Borrowed credibility comes through endorsements. It works but only as long as the celebrity feels authentic. One bad headline and the trust evaporates. This sits as the second-to-the-bottom rung of the trust ladder.

- Analyst → Customer

  White papers and reports provide research-based legitimacy.

They are useful but still distant and sometimes gated or biased by who paid for them.

- Customer → Peer

  Reviews on Yelp or Amazon or comments on LinkedIn matter more because they feel real and unfiltered. But they're still semi-anonymous.

- Customer → Friend

  This is the gold standard. If a friend texts you a plumber's name, you'll almost always call them before you Google. The advice is honest, personal, and rooted in real experience. This is the top of the trust ladder.

The closer you get to the "friend" side of that spectrum, the more credibility you carry. That's where Digital Validation™ operates: in public, visible interactions where others can vouch for you, not just through what you say about yourself.

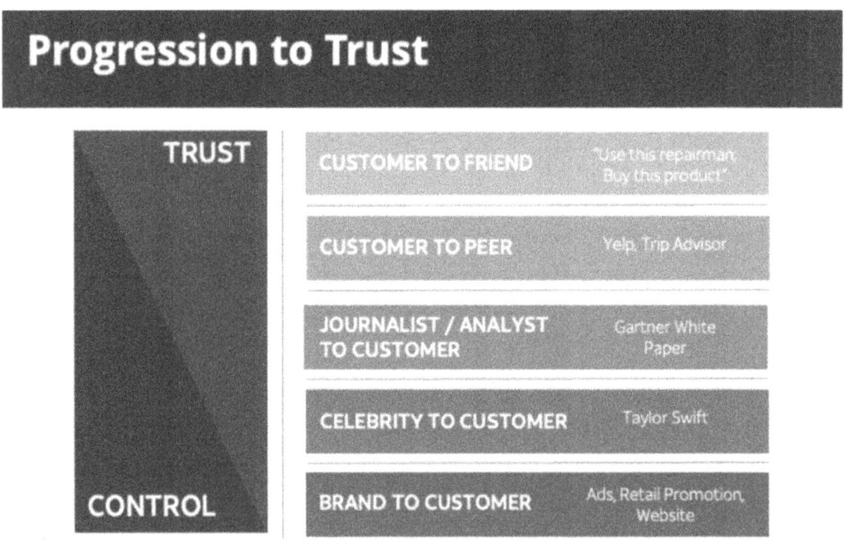

Rules of the Road (Inspired by Dell)

Sometimes people feel unsure about posting and fear that they may get in trouble from their employer

Think of these rules of the road as social media guardrails—the same kind used inside Fortune 500 companies to help employees show up confidently online. They don't restrict your ability to express yourself or build visibility; they simply keep you safely within the lanes so you can focus on driving your career forward.

- *Be helpful. Be respectful. Be human.*

  This is the golden rule of digital presence. Your reputation is shaped more by how you engage than what you post.

- *Never post confidential info or rumors.*

  This is common sense but is often overlooked. A single slip can damage not just your reputation but your employer's.

- *Add "Opinions are my own" in your About section*

  This simple disclaimer sets the boundary between you and your company and gives you room to show personality without blurring lines.

- *Don't feed the trolls. Delete and move on.*

  Engagement is valuable, but not all engagement is worth your energy. Protect your time, tone, and brand.

- *Stay away from divisive topics like politics or religion.*

  Unless it's core to your professional mission, these discussions rarely build bridges in a professional setting.

- *Always assume your current boss and your future boss are watching.*

  Visibility works both ways. Your presence can open doors or quietly close them.

Bottom line:

Stay interested and interesting. Keep it professional, but not robotic.

These rules aren't about stifling your voice; they're about ensuring your voice is heard for the right reasons.

Hashtags (#)—Then vs. Now and How We Got Here

Way back in 2014, hashtags were the GPS for social media. They told people where the conversation was happening and how to find it.

That year, I followed the Social Media Marketing World conference hashtag, #SMMW2014, from my desk in Dallas, wishing I was in San Diego soaking up the sunshine and sessions. Instead, I joined from afar, taking part in social media conversations, asking questions, and meeting people virtually.

By the end of each day, people were tweeting, *"Hey Knox, where are you? Come meet us at happy hour!"*

I'd reply, *"I'm in Dallas."*

On the final day, someone snapped a photo of the conference's engagement board, a leaderboard tracking social media activity tied to the hashtag. To my surprise, I was ranked 5th overall, despite never having set foot in the building.

That little slice of history became a career inflection point. The online engagement led to great conversations and learning, new connections, and interviews with Jay Baer, Mark Schaefer, Ted Rubin, and Guy Kawasaki—connections that helped shape my philosophy around Digital Validation™ years later.

What That Moment Taught Me

That experience proved a simple truth: When you show up online with curiosity, generosity, and consistency, geography doesn't matter; connection does.

Hashtags were just the vehicle. The engine was engagement.

Fast Forward to Today

Now, algorithms drive discovery far more than hashtags. Most platforms (especially LinkedIn) emphasize interest graphs, surfacing content based on relationships, relevance, and behavior rather than a # symbol.

Hashtags today are more like signposts than maps:

- They still help categorize content and signal topics of interest.
- But they no longer guarantee reach or visibility.
- And overuse (the "#lookatme" effect) often hurts credibility more than it helps.

Key Takeaway

The tools change. The principles don't.

Whether it's a hashtag, an algorithm, or the next thing we haven't named yet, what matters is showing up where conversations are happening and adding value once you're there.

Digital Validation™ lives in that consistency: proving credibility through action, not just attention.

Atomizing Your Content

Checklist marketers post once and walk away. Strategic content marketing turns one idea into five weeks of posts. The difference comes down to how you think about content.

Checklist marketing sounds something like this:

Write a blog. → Publish on the company site. →
Post once on LinkedIn. → Done.

It checks the box, but it never moves the needle.

You spent all that time writing something valuable and then let it die after one post. That's not strategy.

Case Study: The $1,000,000 White Paper

A client of mine once spent one million dollars on a white paper. They were a technology manufacturer with a dream of becoming the next *Harvard Business Review* or *McKinsey Quarterly.*

They had the budget, writers, and research muscle and hired a well-known firm to produce beautiful, data-rich studies. Each report cost more than $1,000,000 to create.

When I asked, "How many downloads did it get?" The answer: four. Yes—as in only *four human beings.*

That's when I introduced them to the idea of *atomizing content.*

From Checklist to Campaign

Instead of one post promoting one big piece of content, we broke it apart.

The white paper featured five executives from five different departments.

Each one had three key insights: 15 total data points could easily stand on their own.

We turned those into 15 posts.

Each post highlighted one stat or quote, tagged the relevant team members and linked back to the full paper.

We involved the people mentioned because people connect with people, not brands. (#H2H)

The ripple effect was massive. Employees shared the posts, salespeople commented, product teams jumped in, and the conversation started spreading.

Visibility went from a one-day, one-time post to a five-week campaign.

This time around? More than 2,500 downloads.

Atomizing = Renewable Energy

Content should never be one-and-done. You need to think of it as renewable energy.

Every great blog, podcast, or video can be deconstructed into smaller, story-worthy elements:

- A quote becomes a graphic.
- A stat becomes a post.
- A post becomes a comment thread.
- A conversation becomes a case study.

The key is orchestration: building well-timed, well-connected campaigns that stretch a single idea across multiple touchpoints.

That's not checklist marketing. That's building Digital Validation™.

You're not just publishing content; you're building proof. You're showing consistency, authority, and engagement in action.

Employee Advocacy: Scaling Trust Through People

If atomizing content is about multiplying ideas, employee advocacy is about multiplying voices.

At its core, employee advocacy is the intentional practice of equipping and empowering employees to share company-related content through their own professional networks. It starts with individuals optimizing their LinkedIn profiles and learning how to engage authentically online, and it scales when those individuals become part of a coordinated, well-orchestrated effort.

Why It Matters

- *Trust travels through people, not logos.*

  When employees share stories, insights, and wins, their networks see it as *real*—not as marketing.

- *Visibility compounds.*

  Ten employees with 2,000 followers can each reach 20,000 people—often the right people—compared to a company page with 500.

- *Culture becomes content.*

  Advocacy programs showcase the humans behind the brand, making the organization feel accessible, innovative, and credible.

The Dell Example

When I was at Dell, we built a centralized governance model for employee advocacy programs. That meant clear policies, accessible training, and simple toolkits. We didn't just tell people to post; we taught them how to show up as professionals and ambassadors.

The result: More than 10,000 employees were trained to confidently represent the company online. The ROI wasn't just measured in impressions; it showed up in stronger recruiting, better brand sentiment, improved customer service, and more inbound opportunities for sales teams.

Case Study: The Small Tech Company Example

The same philosophy worked on a smaller scale with a small tech company who was competing against billion-dollar giants like GE. Their corporate LinkedIn page had only a few hundred followers—not exactly a fair fight.

But we flipped the script. We focused on their top four executives, helping each one optimize their profiles, share thought-leadership posts, and engage around company campaigns. Together those four leaders had thousands of professional connections.

The result? Twelve times the reach of the corporate page's posts.

Four people, strategically activated, generated more visibility than an entire brand account ever could.

Key Takeaway

Employee advocacy isn't just social media activity; it's Digital Validation™ at scale.

It's where authenticity meets amplification.

It's how you transform your team from content consumers into brand multipliers.

Start with optimized profiles. Layer in consistent, human content. Then orchestrate campaigns that make everyone a voice for the brand.

That's how you turn employees into your most trusted marketing channel.

Outside Perspective

"The most underutilized marketing and product development resources in any company are its own employees."

—John Starkweather

The core belief is simple: Your employees are not just brand representatives; they *are the brand*. When equipped and empowered, they can reach audiences with more authenticity, trust, and impact than any corporate channel.

The above case study underscores this.

I am considering exploring this topic, employee advocacy, much more deeply in a second book. If you think this is a worthy endeavor, drop me a note on social media! But for now, remember this: Your most powerful marketing engine is likely already on your payroll.

The Power of Story: How She Supply Turned Connection into Contribution

Facts tell. Stories sell.

Or, numbers inform. Stories inspire and connect.

Case Study: She Supply

She Supply is a Dallas-area nonprofit that provides feminine hygiene products to women in need across the five North Texas counties. Their mission is deeply human, but like many small nonprofits, they were struggling to break through the noise of larger, better-known organizations—especially during North Texas Giving Day, an event where the heavy hitters such as Salvation Army, SPCA, and Susan G. Komen tend to dominate donor attention.

When we started working with She Supply, their online fundraising total sat around $2,800.

Twelve months later, during North Texas Giving Day, they raised $18,700.

The difference wasn't a bigger ad budget or flashier graphics. It was *Digital Validation™* in action and the power of story.

From Generic Appeals to Personal Narratives

We began by helping the volunteer board realize something simple but profound: Every one of them had a *reason* for being there.

Some had been single mothers. Some had grown up in poverty. Some had volunteered in shelters and seen the need firsthand.

Those individual "whys" became the foundation for a new kind of campaign, one built on authenticity and personal connection.

Instead of generic posts asking for donations, board members began sharing their own stories on social media and LinkedIn: why they cared, how She Supply made a difference, and what it meant to see dignity restored through something as small as access to basic products.

Each story was a digital handshake: human, relatable, and real.

The Ripple Effect

The results were immediate and measurable:

- Engagement spiked as new audiences discovered the organization through board members' personal networks.
- Donations multiplied sixfold, from $2,800 to $18,700.
- Most importantly, She Supply began to compete—and win—against the bigger, more established nonprofit brands.
- And word spread. More and more people learned about the need for She Supply.

That's the power of story. It builds trust faster than any statistic. It turns a "cause" into a connection.

Key Takeaway

Whether you're a nonprofit, a start-up, or a Fortune 500 brand, stories are your greatest currency of trust.

People connect with the *why.*

Digital Validation™ amplifies that. You're not just broadcasting a message; you're building a movement, one authentic story at a time.

Rules of the Road: Keep It Simple

Once you start showing up online by sharing ideas, engaging with others, and building your digital presence, it's important to understand where the guardrails are. These guidelines, inspired by our work at Dell, were tested inside a Fortune 500 company and trained to more than 10,000 employees around the world. The goal was simple: empower people to show up professionally, confidently, and responsibly.

Here's the same framework I teach today:

Keep It Simple

- Be transparent. Let people know who you are and who you work for.
- Protect information. Never share confidential or financial data.
- Be helpful. Add value through insights, not inside information.
- Have fun. Bring personality. Just keep it professional.

Highly Recommended

- Add "Opinions are my own" to your LinkedIn About or Summary section. It's a simple way to clarify that you speak for yourself, not your employer. Stay positive, upbeat, helpful, and inquisitive.
- Tone matters as much as content. People remember how you make them feel. Be interested *and* interesting.
- Engage with others' ideas, share your perspective, and stay curious.

What Not to Post

Think of this as your "digital common-sense checklist." These aren't about fear; they're about protecting trust, your reputation, and your company's credibility.

- Do not share company secrets, financials, or unannounced projects.
- Do not make claims about your company's services (or competitors').
- Avoid topics under litigation or any internal rumors.
- Do not speak on behalf of your employer unless it's part of your role.
- Do not "feed the trolls." Delete, block, and move on.
- Avoid politics, religion, and divisive topics that derail professional trust.

The bottom line: Keep it simple, stay human, and protect trust.

When in doubt, ask yourself: *Would I be comfortable seeing this quoted on the front page of LinkedIn News tomorrow?*

If the answer is yes, post away.

Transition to Final Thoughts

These bonus frameworks and stories are meant to be tools you can return to again and again. They're not the main event; they're the momentum builders.

In the next and final chapter, we'll bring it all together: your story, strategy, and sustained digital presence.

QR Code

CHAPTER 14
Final Thoughts

You made it.

In a noisy, distracted world, showing up with intention is no small task. Most people never finish what they start, but you did. That's when the change truly begins.

I am proud of you.

Thank you.

Thank you for investing your time, focus, and energy into this journey. I don't take that lightly. This book wasn't written to be clever or trendy. It was written to be useful, to give you a practical roadmap to shape your digital presence with intention and confidence.

And if you're here, at the very end, you've already done something most people won't: You've taken that first step to owning your narrative.

What You've Learned

Let's distill everything down to the essentials: your quick reference guide to Digital Validation™.

- Your digital footprint matters. People *will* Google you.
- LinkedIn is not your resume. It's so much more. It's your professional storefront.
- Personal branding says, "Look at me." Professional branding or Digital Validation™ says, "I'm here to add value. I know what I'm talking about. Here's the proof."
- Add value. Don't just broadcast.
- Visibility is not about going viral; it is about showing up consistently with value and intention.
- A strong content framework builds trust and credibility when it's implemented consistently.
- The real growth hack is engagement.
- None of this is about chasing perfection. It's about being findable, believable, and human.
- You have downloaded your LinkedIn Scorecard and taken a hard view of where you stood and how you needed to improve it.
- Conversations drive relationships and greater visibility.

Every one of these principles has been tested in the trenches with executives, entrepreneurs, students, nonprofits, small business owners, and sales teams who needed more clarity, confidence, and visibility.

Remember: Without engagement, social media isn't social. It's just noise.

From Strategy to Action—Making It Stick

Reading this book is a milestone, but the real transformation happens in the *doing*.

Here's a simple rhythm to keep you moving toward being seen and keeping your Digital Validation™ practice alive.

- Weekly
  - Share a post at least once.
  - Comment meaningfully on five posts.
  - Send one well-thought-out DM to reconnect or build a new relationship.
- Monthly
  - Track your progress.
    - Did your posts generate comments and conversations?
    - Did your comments turn into more engagement?
    - How often are you DMing and connecting / reconnecting?
  - Evaluate how your content is performing. Are certain posts or topics resonating more than others?
- Quarterly
  - Track your progress as before, comparing the longer horizons.
  - Identify new people with whom to connect with or drive visibility.
  - Review your headline and about section and determine whether they need to be updated.

Small steps create momentum, and momentum is everything.

You don't need to do everything at once. Start where you are, build your rhythm, and let consistency compound.

Stay Connected

Your digital presence is not a one-time project. It is a living practice, just like leading a healthy lifestyle. Make it a habit. And remember the *crawl – walk – run* framework to build these habits.

If you want to keep learning, growing, and seeing what works in real time, I post about what I'm working on regularly:

- www.knoxkeith.com/my-thoughts
- Instagram: @knoxknox
- Newsletter—see QR Code section

You are not in this alone. I'll be right there in the feed with you.

What's Next—A Glimpse into the Future

This book is about owning your story. The next one is about what happens when teams do it together. When employees become the most trusted voice of a brand, everything changes. That's the movement we will explore next.

It's about *employee advocacy*: how to turn your people into your most trusted and impactful set of marketing tools.

We did it at Dell. We did it for a division of AT&T. We did it for start-ups and nonprofits. We did for B2B and B2C companies. We did it for sales teams.

Next, I want to show you how to build that kind of culture and community, too.

If Digital Validation™ is about owning your story, then employee advocacy is about amplifying it together.

After all, people trust people more than they trust faceless brands. (Remember the progression to trust slide from Chapter 13.)

Now It's Your Turn

Here's the truth:

No one can "build your brand" for you.

Not a ghostwriter. Not an agency. Not AI.

You already have everything you need. You are the product. You are the signal.

So keep moving forward. Keep refining. Keep showing up. Keep adding value. Keep being consistent. And you will be seen.

It's what worked for me. It's what worked for my clients. And it can work for you. But only if you apply it.

Call to Action

If you only do one thing after reading this book, *take action this week.* Optimize your LinkedIn profile. Post once. Comment once.

Just start! That's how momentum begins.

QR CODE

Index

Symbols

A

B

C

D

E

F

www.ingramcontent.com/pod-product-compliance
Ingram Content Group UK Ltd.
Pitfield, Milton Keynes, MK11 3LW, UK
UKHW060126010826
14089UKWH00020B/263/J

9 798994 194805